BOSTON RED SOX

Where Have You Gone?

STEVE BUCKLEY

www.SportsPublishingLLC.com

ISBN: 1-58261-961-1

Publishers: Peter L. Bannon and Joseph J. Bannon Sr.
Senior managing editor: Susan M. Moyer
Acquisitions editor: Mike Pearson
Developmental editor: Dean Miller
Art director: K. Jeffrey Higgerson
Book design: Jennifer L. Polson
Dust jacket design: Kenneth J. O'Brien
Project manager: Kathryn R. Holleman
Imaging: Kenneth J. O'Brien, Heidi Norsen, and Dustin Hubbart
Photo editor: Erin Linden-Levy
Vice president of sales and marketing: Kevin King
Media and promotions managers: Courtney Hainline (regional),
    Randy Fouts (national), Maurey Williamson (print)

Printed in the United States of America

Sports Publishing L.L.C.
804 North Neil Street
Champaign, IL 61820

Phone: 1-877-424-2665
Fax: 217-363-2073
Web site: www.SportsPublishingLLC.com

*In memory
of Ken Coleman,
THE voice of the Red Sox*

*He always said that being there is twice the fun.
Left unsaid was that Kenny's skill
behind the microphone always made it
seem as though we were there.*

CONTENTS

ACKNOWLEDGMENTS

W hen Ray Culp was asked to be interviewed for this book, the first response from the old righthander was to offer up an apology.

"I'm just not a very good storyteller," he said. "I don't think I'm very interesting and I don't think I can give you what you're looking for."

And then Ray Culp proceeded to talk for the next, oh, 45 minutes, waxing nostalgic about his baseball career. Boring? Hardly. This is a man whose sense of humor is such that he once named a company after his paltry lifetime batting average: 123 Inc.

That's my way of stating the obvious: This book would not be possible without the cooperation of the 50 ex-Red Sox players whose stories appear on these pages. They talked about baseball, but they also talked about so much more—their lives, their families, their heartbreak. When Jim Pagliaroni told me about the auto accident that nearly ended his life, or when Lee Tinsley talked about his ailing father, it served as a reminder that ballplayers, famous or not, are just ordinary people who happen also to be blessed with a good fastball, a keen batting eye or a slick glove.

Thanks also must be extended to longtime Red Sox executive Dick Bresciani and to Debbie Matson, director of publications for the Sox. Even in the age of the internet, it's still hard to track down oldtime ballplayers who have faded from the public eye. But Dick and Debbie provided names, addresses and telephone numbers, along with some photographs that might have been impossible to uncover through other means.

Andrew Green, who is playing baseball at Amherst College until he lands his first job as a big-league general manager, provided a huge assist in the procurement of photographs, as did my pal J.C. Bejoian and his gang at the Alba Press.

It's helpful when the people on the publishing end share your interest in the material. As such, my thanks go out to the folks at Sports Publishing LLC., especially Dean Miller, who had all this stuff in his hands before you did.

Finally, thanks to the ever-obsessed citizens of Red Sox Nation. If they don't have their passion, I don't have a book.

INTRODUCTION

On a rainy August evening in 1994, after yet another labor crisis had shut down Major League Baseball, more than a thousand people showed up at a tiny ballfield in Cambridge, Massachusetts, for an event that was meant to celebrate the very game that the big boys seemed intent on destroying.

The affair was called The Oldtime Baseball Game, and I was one of its organizers. And while the big leagues did return in 1995—there was, in the end, no ruination of the game—we decided to keep staging our quaint summertime celebration of baseball.

Over the years, many of the region's top high school and college players have participated in the game. We began to invite former big-leaguers to play, with the likes of Mike Pagliarulo, Jim Corsi and Oil Can Boyd participating. We've had Joe Morgan, Johnny Pesky and Lennie Merullo as managers. We've invited Dick "The Monster" Radatz to throw out the first pitch. We eventually landed a corporate sponsor, and even found a sugar daddy to pay for a dazzling collection of oldtime uniforms that are used just once a year for our game.

What the Oldtime Baseball Game has taught us is that hardball and philanthropy mix well together: The event has raised nearly a half-million dollars for various local charities. But it also has given us a wonderful grassroots baseball education, as, each year, we discover new bits and pieces of information about the real-life players whose old-style uniforms are represented in the game.

When I was given an opportunity to write this book, my first thought was to contact the committee members of the Oldtime Baseball Game and ask one simple question: If you could pick one ex-Red Sox player to be included, who would that player be?

Bill Novelline, a big-hearted businessman from Andover, Massachusetts, who still has a child's love of all matters baseball, did not even hesitate.

"Lou Stringer," he said.

I had to confess I had never heard of Lou Stringer.

"He played for the Red Sox in the late 40s, early 50s," said Novelline. "He was a reserve infielder. I met him at Fenway Park when I was a kid, and I never forgot it. I'd love to read what happened to him."

And that's why you'll learn about Lou Stringer in this book: More than a half-century ago, he took the time to be nice to a little kid. That's the magic of baseball, isn't it? Though casual fans remember the stars, it's the diehards who bestow a sort of immortality on the Lou Stringers of the world.

The other committee members—Marlinda Langone (whose son, Steve, plays in the minor leagues for the Red Sox), Ben Weiss, Andrew Novelline, Dave and Sue Leibovitz and the great and powerful J.C. Bejoian—were also asked to submit the names of players they wished to see included in this book.

And you're about to read their stories, and many more. In the end, I hope you'll agree that many ballplayers make for even better copy after the lights have dimmed.

Steve Buckley,
Boston, Massachusetts
January 14, 2005

Where Have You Gone?

BOSTON RED SOX

Where Have You Gone?

FRED LYNN

It was the most talked-about moment of the Red Sox' 2004 regular season: catcher Jason Varitek jawing in front of the plate with the Yankees' Alex Rodriguez, a dispute that led to Varitek smooshing his catcher's mitt into A-Rod's handsome face.

As the benches emptied and the crowd roared, it brought back a lot of memories to a man standing in the so-called "Legends Suite" at Fenway Park.

"I guess nothing changes," said Fred Lynn, laughing a little as he watched the melee that was unfolding down on the field. "We hated the Yankees back when I was playing here, and it looks like the tradition is continuing."

But while some things never change, some things do change. Consider, for example, the mere fact that Lynn was on hand for the game, having been flown to Boston from his California home—by the Red Sox—to make an appearance at the highfalutin Legends Suite. The irony here is that in 1980 the Red Sox traded Fred Lynn to the California Angels because they didn't want to pay him. Now, under fresh, new ownership, the Red Sox were paying him just to stand around and talk baseball with some high-rolling fans.

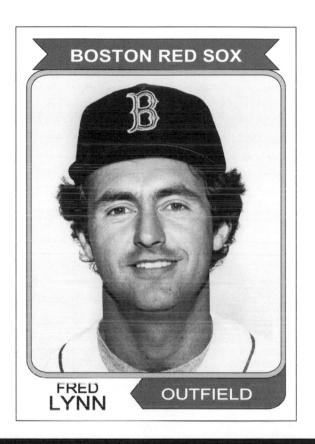

BOSTON RED SOX

FRED
LYNN

OUTFIELD

FRED LYNN
Seasons with Red Sox: 1974-1980

Best Season With Red Sox: 1975 (Rookie of the Year, MVP)

• Games: 145 • Batting Average: .331 • At Bats: 528 • Hits: 175 •
• Runs: 103 • Home Runs: 21 • RBIs: 105 • Slugging Percentage: .566 •

It was, of course, a bad move by the Red Sox to trade Fred Lynn. But it also was a bad move for Lynn's career, as the outfielder would never again be the same player he had been during his mostly carefree days at Fenway Park.

"I never wanted to leave here," said Lynn. "I would have been happy to spend my entire career with the Red Sox. Why would I want to go anywhere else when I was hitting .350 lifetime here?"

Lynn was an overnight success in his rookie season in 1975, hitting .331 with 21 home runs and 105 RBIs. In helping to power the Red Sox to the World Series, he became the first player to win both Rookie of the Year and Most Valuable Player honors, and in 1979 he had an even better season, hitting .333 with 39 home runs and 122 RBIs.

But Haywood Sullivan, who had become an owner of the team following the 1976 death of Thomas Yawkey, had made it his stated goal to hold the line on high contracts. One way to accomplish his mission was to trade Lynn to the California Angels. More accurately, he gave Lynn away, acquiring two players past their prime (pitcher Frank Tanana and outfielder Joe Rudi) and a young righthander (Jim Dorsey) who would make only four big-league appearances for the Red Sox.

After his years with the Red Sox, Lynn became a baseball nomad. After four seasons with the Angels—including being named MVP of the 1982 American League Championship Series, and his 1983 All-Star Game grand slam off Atlee Hammaker—Lynn moved on to the Orioles, Tigers and Padres. He retired in 1990 with a .283 average and 306 home runs.

There are those who believe Lynn would have been a Hall of Famer had the Red Sox not traded him. Yet the years after baseball have been kind to Lynn. More's the point, he has been kind to his years: "Well, I weighed 182 pounds when I broke into the big leagues, and I weigh 181 pounds now," said the energetic, youthful-looking Lynn, who was born in 1952. "I got up to 195 while I was playing, but then I discovered running, and I kept running off all my weight training. But these days my knees won't allow me to run as much as I'd like."

After his playing days, Lynn tried his hand in a variety of fields, including the clothing business.

"I did some work with a clothing manufacturer and I tried to get them involved with Major League Baseball, but it didn't work out," Lynn said. "If you know anything about licensing, then you know it can be a tough deal. It was a David vs. Goliath kind of thing, and it didn't make it."

These days, Lynn is involved in corporate outings for Major League Baseball, handling such clients as John Hancock. He also makes numerous public appearances, such as his Legends Suite duties with the Red Sox.

The man is perfect for such occasions—not just because of his fame as a ballplayer, but because Fred Lynn, then and now, mixes well with diverse groups of people.

Consider, for example, Lynn's long, close relationship with the late Sherm Feller, for many years the public address announcer at Fenway Park. It was, to put it mildly, an odd pairing. Lynn was young, dashing and famous; Feller was an old, rumpled, unmade bed of a man, and more interested in late-night diners than the fast lane of big-league baseball.

Asked how this hardball Odd Couple was formed, Lynn pointed out toward center field, his old stomping grounds.

"You see that speaker out there that's built into the center-field wall? I stood in front of that speaker every night," he said. "Sherm would turn on his microphone to make an announcement, and then he'd turn it off, so to speak. But he'd screw it up, and the thing was still on, and he'd start mumbling to whoever was up there with him. He'd be speaking just loud enough to be heard by someone who might be standing in front of that speaker—which was me.

"And I'd see him in the clubhouse after the game, and I'd say to him, 'Hey, Sherm, turn off the microphone when you're up there babbling. I can hear everything you say.' And of course it would keep on happening. And that's how I got to know him so well."

It was an unusual, but very real, friendship. It also became something of a business arrangement: Feller was an accomplished writer of music whose credits included the 1958 pop hit "Summertime, Summertime," and, later in life, he took a stab at composing a symphony in memory of John F. Kennedy. Lynn provided financing for the copyrights to what became "Ode to JFK," and was very proud the night Feller's creation was performed at Boston Symphony Hall.

Fred Lynn has two grown children. He and his second wife, Natalie, a former Boston television producer, live in Carlsbad, California.

Where Have You Gone?

BILLY MacLEOD

If you've seen the classic baseball film *Field of Dreams*, you may remember the scene filmed at Fenway Park showing Kevin Costner and James Earl Jones having a discussion about the '60s as they head for their seats.

The scene was filmed on a ramp that was no longer in everyday use at the old ballpark, a ramp that, because of various renovations over the years, is literally a passage to nowhere.

That is, until 2004, when a plan was hatched to use the ramp as a place where fans could meet and interact with former Red Sox players who would be brought in for just such occasions. And so it was that Fenway Park's "Autograph Alley" was born.

On most days, the players are well-known stars from the not-too-distant past. A Rico Petrocelli, perhaps, or maybe a Dick Radatz.

But on Sunday, September 5, 2004, before the Red Sox closed out a three-game series against the Texas Rangers, the man of the hour at Autograph Alley was a cheerful, white-haired man whose name—Billy MacLeod—was undoubtedly foreign to most of the fans who gathered in the Alley.

Billy MacLeod? He pitched just two games for the Red Sox. Called up to the big leagues in September of 1962 after a decent season in the

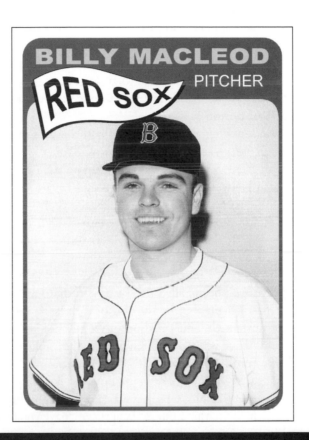

BILLY MacLEOD
Year with Red Sox: 1961

Best Season with Red Sox: 1961

• Games: 2 • Record: 0-1 • ERA: 5.40 • Innings Pitched: 1⅔ •
• Hits Allowed: 4 • Strikeouts: 2 • Walks: 1 •

minor leagues, the 20-year-old lefty faced the Detroit Tigers in a relief stint at Tiger Stadium, and then pitched against the Washington Senators, also on the road.

And that was that. He was back in the minors in 1963, and continued pitching until the spring of '68, when he was released by the Chicago White Sox. He never pitched in the big leagues again.

But what made MacLeod's trip to Autograph Alley a special event is that, finally, after all these years, he was being invited to Fenway Park by the Red Sox. And let's stop right here to point out that MacLeod is a Massachusetts native—born and raised in Gloucester, the famous fishing village north of Boston.

"When I was growing up, a trip to Boston was something you planned a month in advance," said MacLeod. "You didn't just go to Boston. It was an event. So when I was called up in '62, I was hoping I'd get into a game at Fenway.

"There was one game—against the Yankees—when I was warming up. The place was packed. My family was there. I had friends there. I don't remember exactly what happened, but the inning ended, and the situation changed, and I never got into the game.

"As I look back on it, I have mixed feelings," he said. "See, I probably shouldn't have even been called up. I was 8-6 that year with Seattle in the Pacific Coast League, but by the end of the season my elbow was hurting. Plus, I was young, and I had only two pitches, a fastball and a curve. But would I have wanted to pitch against the Yankees that day at Fenway, with my family there? You bet."

But the mystery of MacLeod's career is not why he was promoted to the big leagues in 1962, but why he was not brought up in 1965. Pitching for Pittsfield in the Eastern League in '65, MacLeod was a dynamo, posting an 18-0 record. Counting his final four decisions of the '64 season, he won 22 consecutive games. Yet the Red Sox not only didn't promote MacLeod to the big leagues during the season, they didn't bring him up in September, after his minor-league campaign had ended.

"And I was a much better pitcher by '65," MacLeod said. "I had learned to throw a change-up by then, and I had a slider. Plus, my elbow was fine. I was ready to return to the big leagues."

Raised in a blue-collar family—his mother worked in the Gloucester High School cafeteria and his father ran a labeling machine at Gorton's Seafoods—MacLeod accepted a $12,000 bonus to sign with the Red Sox in 1960 after fashioning a 9-0 regular-season record his final year at Gloucester High School.

"When I got my bonus money, the first thing I did was what all kids do when they get a bonus—I went out and bought a car," MacLeod said. "I bought a Valliant. And the thing is, I didn't even have my driver's license yet. Can you imagine that? No driver's license, and I have a brand new car. Go figure."

Because it wasn't until July that MacLeod signed with the Red Sox, the team decided to hold him back from beginning his minor-league career until the following spring. Instead, he spent the rest of the summer working out with the big-league club when it was home.

"And remember, it was 1960, Ted Williams' last year," MacLeod said. "There I was, in uniform, on the same field as Ted Williams, throwing batting practice to the regulars."

Did he throw BP to Ted Williams?

"Not a chance," he said. "They weren't going to have an 18-year-old lefthander throwing batting practice to Ted Williams. I didn't even go near him. I was too bashful."

Following the end of his baseball career, MacLeod worked in a variety of fields. He ran a restaurant for a while. He tended bar. He was manager of the Cottage Park Yacht Club in Winthrop. He eventually became assistant head teller at the National Brand Bank in Marblehead.

As for MacLeod's family, we are talking about a man who is remarkably consistent. During his first marriage, he fathered a son and twin girls. Married a second time, he fathered a son . . . and twin girls.

On the day he appeared at Autograph Alley, he was accompanied by his second set of twins, Katie and Jennie, born in 1989.

"It was nice to share this with them," he said. "And it was nice to be able to walk into Fenway Park and be remembered as a guy who pitched for the Boston Red Sox."

Where Have You Gone?

RICK MILLER

Reached in December, 2004, a couple of weeks before Christmas, Rick Miller was standing on a hill near the home of his in-laws, being ever so careful not to move too much, lest his cell phone signal be eaten up by the late-night New Hampshire sky.

"Cell phone reception around here is terrible," he said. "When we're here, sometimes I just pick a time to go on top of the hill to make all my calls. Other than that, people can't reach me."

When we caught up with Miller, a Michigan native who has long since settled in New Hampshire, he was in the town of Charlestown, near the Vermont border, making repairs on the home of his wife's parents, Cecil and Lee Fisk. This is the home in which his wife, Janet, grew up, as did Miller's brother-in-law, Hall of Fame catcher Carlton Fisk, and now, with winter fast approaching, the former Red Sox outfielder was racing the weatherman to get his work done.

"Nothing major," he said. "I'm doing some wallpapering, fixing some cracks here and there, doing some cleaning up, that kind of thing."

It's not very glamorous work for a guy who spent 15 seasons in the big leagues, including two long stretches with the Red Sox, but this is the way Miller prefers things to be. He and Janet live in a home that sits on a lake in New London, New Hampshire, and he's happy to point out

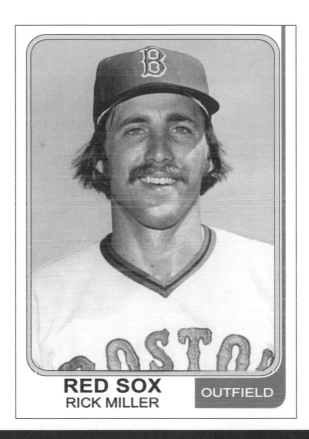

RED SOX
RICK MILLER
OUTFIELD

RICK MILLER
Years with Red Sox: 1971-1977, 1981-1985

Best Season with Red Sox: 1973

• Games: 143 • Batting Average: .261 • At Bats: 441 • Hits: 115 •
• Runs: 65 • Home Runs: 6 • RBIs: 43 • Slugging Percentage: .372 •

that "I have a view to die for, but in the wintertime I have the driveway from hell."

Born in Grand Rapids, Michigan, on April 19, 1948, Miller starred in baseball at Michigan State, where one of his teammates was future big-league star Steve Garvey. Selected by the Red Sox in the second round of the 1969 June amateur draft, it took him only two years to make it to the big leagues, as he was added to the roster in September, 1971.

Miller did *not* hit a home run in his first big-league at-bat, and didn't tear up American League pitching during a September call-up. Yet anyone who saw Miller play for the Red Sox in September of 1971 will never forget what they saw: Night after night, game after game, Miller made sensational catch after sensational catch, and it didn't hurt him any that in his 33 at-bats he managed 11 hits, a .333 average, along with his first major-league home run.

"I always felt I played the game the way it should be played," said Miller, and it's true. Though he was never a star, he was a solid defensive player, including a Gold Glove season with the California Angels in 1978, and in 1972, despite appearing in just 89 games with the Red Sox, he was voted the team's "Unsung Hero" by the Boston chapter of the Baseball Writers Association of America.

Granted free agency after the 1977 season, Miller signed with the Angels. He spent three years with the Angels, including the 1979 season, the best of his career: He hit .293 in 120 games, helping the Angels to a first-place finish in the American League West.

Traded back to the Red Sox, Miller finished out his career in Boston, playing five more seasons. Most of his time back in Boston was pleasant. But it didn't end as well as it had begun. By 1985 he was a bit player, appearing in just 41 games. He ended his career with the same batting average with which he began his career—.333—but with a difference: In 1971, he had 33 at-bats in less than a month, but in 1985 he had 45 at-bats spread out over a season.

"I don't know what I did, or what I said, but John McNamara just never had any use for me," he said, referring to the former Red Sox manager. "I later found out he wanted to release me in spring training, but Joe Morgan, who was a coach at the time, asked him who his fourth outfielder would be, who his left-handed pinch-hitter would be, and so on. He ended up keeping me, but I never played.

"McNamara was a coach for a while when I was with the Angels, so maybe he formed some kind of impression of me back then," he said. "But I don't know what that could have been. I always prided myself in the way I carried myself as a major-league ballplayer. That was always important to me. Maybe I'll meet McNamara one of these days and he can tell me what the problem was he had with me."

Miller talked with the Red Sox about a coaching position when his career ended, but, as he put it, "That season left a sour taste in my stomach. I needed to get away from baseball for a while."

He did return to the game in 1991 as a minor-league scout with the San Francisco Giants, but he eventually settled in New Hampshire and went into business for himself. Among his ventures was a baseball camp, which he had started with some of his old Red Sox teammates. He still works as a private baseball tutor, and in the spring he is the hitting coach at Colby-Sawyer College. But it's not like Miller has to travel very far: Colby-Sawyer's beautiful campus is just a few miles from Miller's house in New London.

Miller probably never would have found the peace and tranquility of New Hampshire had he not been roommates with Carlton Fisk while the two men played for the Red Sox. Fisk introduced his kid sister Janet to Miller during spring training one year, and the two became pen pals, trading letters and postcards. It wasn't until nearly two years later that they began to date.

They have a son, Joshua, who now lives in Lake Tahoe, California, and works in the ski industry.

Where Have You Gone?

CARROLL HARDY

For more than 40 years, nary a month has passed without Carroll Hardy opening his mailbox and finding another letter from some far-flung fan who wants him to sign a baseball card, or perhaps a baseball or a photograph.

"And I've done some card shows," said Hardy. "I did one in Boston a couple of years ago. You wouldn't believe how much attention I received. It was pretty impressive."

Not bad for a career .225 hitter who scratched out parts of eight seasons in the big leagues with four different teams. But now and forever, Carroll Hardy holds a singular place in the history of the Red Sox, along with making him the answer to one of baseball's most commonly asked trivia questions: Who is the only man ever to pinch hit for Ted Williams?

"And the funny thing is that, when it happened, I didn't think it was a big deal," said Hardy, who lives outside Denver with his wife, Jan. "A couple of years later I got a call from a reporter who asked me about being the only man to pinch hit for Ted Williams, and I have to say I was surprised. And I've been hearing about it ever since. It won't go away."

Born in Sturgis, South Dakota, on May 18, 1933, Carroll Hardy seemed destined for a career not in baseball, but in football. He was a

CARROLL HARDY
Years with Red Sox: 1960-1962

Best Season with Red Sox: 1961

• Games: 85 • Batting Average: .263 • At Bats: 281 • Hits: 74 •
• Runs: 46 • Home Runs: 3 • RBIs: 36 • Slugging Percentage: .381 •

star tailback for the University of Colorado, after which he logged a season in the National Football League with the San Francisco 49ers, catching four touchdown passes. But he wound up signing with the Cleveland Indians as an outfielder, and he made his major-league debut on April 15, 1958.

The stage for his brush with history—and sports trivia—was set on June 13, 1960, when the Indians traded him to the Red Sox, along with catcher Russ Nixon, for outfielder Marty Keough and pitcher Ted Bowsfield.

Now, let's fast forward to September 20, 1960, and the last days of Ted Williams's glorious big-league career. It was the Red Sox vs. the Orioles at Baltimore's Memorial Stadium, with Hardy sitting in the dugout as a spare part—until Williams had to leave the game after fouling a pitch off his foot.

"Hardy, grab a bat," hollered Red Sox manager Mike Higgins.

"I was coming off the bench cold, without a chance to stretch," said Hardy. "There was a runner on first base. I figured I would drop a bunt, and, if nothing else, I'd move the runner up to second base."

So Hardy dropped his bunt. And Brooks Robinson, the young Hall of Fame-bound third baseman for the Orioles, gobbled it up and turned a double play.

"Had I known the greatest third baseman in baseball history was on the field," said Hardy, "maybe I wouldn't have bunted."

It was not the first time, or the last time, that Hardy would be linked with baseball history. A little more than a week later, when Williams homered in his last big-league at-bat, it was Hardy who replaced Teddy Ballgame in left field. And in 1961, Hardy was asked on three occasions to pinch-hit for rookie outfielder Carl Yastrzemski, thus becoming the only man to hit for the two greatest left fielders in Red Sox history.

"I had better luck hitting for Yaz," said Hardy. "I had two doubles in those three at-bats."

Hardy can also do some boasting about his first home run in the big leagues. It took place on May 18, 1958, his rookie season with the Indians. He was pinch hitting for Roger Maris, who three years later with the Yankees would break Babe Ruth's single-season home run record.

And then there was October 1, 1967, one of the greatest days in Red Sox history. It was on this day that the 100-to-1 longshot Red Sox defeated the Minnesota Twins to clinch at least a tie for first place in the

American League, and then claimed the pennant later that afternoon when the Angels defeated the Detroit Tigers.

Hardy's role in all this? When Rich Rollins popped out to shortstop Rico Petrocelli for the game's final out, it was none other than Carroll Hardy kneeling in the on-deck circle. He had been out of the big leagues since 1964, kicking around the minors, and by '67 he was playing for the Twins' Triple-A club in Denver club. The Twins added him to their big-league roster in September, and he had just eight at-bats, getting three hits.

In the top of the ninth, Twins manager Cal Ermer had him in the on-deck circle to hit for pitcher Mudcat Grant.

"But then Rollins popped out, and the place went crazy," Hardy said. "There were people coming on the field from every direction, and all I was thinking was, 'I gotta get out of here.'"

As things happened, it would have been Hardy's last major-league at-bat. When the season ended, the Twins asked him to manage their St. Cloud team in the old Northern League. But the problem was that Hardy, who needed just a few more weeks of service time to get five full seasons in the big leagues for pension purposes, wanted to keep playing.

"So I met with (Twins owner) Calvin Griffith, and they made me a deal," Hardy said. "If I managed St. Cloud, they'd put me on the big-league roster at the end of the season. And that's just what happened. I managed St. Cloud, and we did well, and then I reported to the Twins and threw batting practice for a couple of weeks."

Hardy's '68 St. Cloud Sox performed well, registering a 43-27 record and finishing atop the standings in the Northern League. Perhaps Hardy was headed for a long career as a big-league manager.

But no. Instead, Hardy returned to football, taking a job with the Denver Broncos, for whom he worked in a variety of scouting capacities for more than 22 years, until, he said, "Dan Reeves came in and moved me out so he could give my job to one of his college buddies."

Carroll Hardy lives in comfortable retirement in the Denver area.

"Not a bad life," he said. "And I'll tell you, for a .225 hitter I sure got in the middle of some things, don't you think?"

BILLY CONIGLIARO

For years, Billy Conigliaro never set foot inside Fenway Park. It had nothing to do with bitterness, or unresolved issues with management, or geography. No, Conigliaro was still living in the Boston area, within easy access of the old ballyard he once called home, but Conigliaro was one of those players whose life, along with family circumstances, took him in a different direction.

He worked as a professional photographer. He opened a camera store. He ran a country club. And then he started to renovate old houses, eventually earning his contractor's license.

But in recent years, Conigliaro has started to re-emerge as a member of the Red Sox family. He began making semi-regular appearances at Fenway Park in 2002 and 2003, including sessions in "Autograph Alley," where Red Sox players from the past are brought in to meet the fans and tell stories about the old days.

Conigliaro has even considered returning to the game as a coach.

"It's something that crossed my mind a few years back and I would like to do," said Conigliaro, who, though he turned 57 during the 2004 season, looks significantly younger than that. "The game was always a part of me, even when I wasn't around it. And once I started coming to Fenway Park again, I started thinking about getting back into baseball."

BILLY CONIGLIARO
Seasons with Red Sox: 1969-1971

Best Season with Red Sox: 1970

• Games: 114 • Batting Average: .271 • At Bats: 398 • Hits: 108 •
• Runs: 59 • Home Runs: 18 • RBIs: 58 • Slugging Percentage: .462 •

Why the change? Friends and family members point to Conigliaro's wife, Keisha, who became the first woman to pull the career bachelor down the matrimonial aisle. Just 25 years old when she married Conigliaro on October 19, 2002, she is said to have nudged her husband back toward baseball, a game he played with passion from the day he was drafted by the Red Sox in 1965 to the day he was released by the Oakland A's during the last week of spring training in 1974.

But there's more to the story. Let's remember that Conigliaro is the younger brother of the late Tony Conigliaro, a sensational Red Sox slugger in the early and mid 1960s and was in the process of forging a Hall of Fame career when he was beaned by a Jack Hamilton fastball in 1967.

The Tony C. story has been oft-told: He made a dramatic comeback with the Red Sox in 1969, the same year his younger brother Billy made his major-league debut. In 1970, Tony C. hit a career-high 36 home runs, but the Red Sox, sensing that his eyesight was deteriorating, traded him to the California Angels. He quit the Angels in 1971, made another comeback with the Red Sox in 1975, and then retired for good. In 1982, after auditioning for a job as a Red Sox television analyst, Tony C. suffered a massive heart attack as he was being driven to the airport.

The man doing the driving that day was Billy Conigliaro.

Tony C. was physically and mentally crippled by the attack. He lingered for nearly eight years, never really regaining consciousness, before dying on February 24, 1990.

In the foreword to *Tony C: The Triumph and Tragedy of Tony Conigliaro*, Billy Conigliaro writes about the anxious moments after his brother's heart attack and the rush to a nearby hospital: "If I had to do it all over again—knowing now what everyone, especially Tony, went through during the eight agonizingly frustrating years of round-the-clock care before his death in 1990—I would pull over to the side of the road and just say good-bye to the brother I loved. This would have saved Tony the pain, the torture, and horrible existence he would suffer."

So, as we write these words about ex-Red Sox players and what they have done in their years after baseball, it is important to understand what Billy Conigliaro went through during those eight years following his older brother's heart attack. Instead of enjoying a sort of post-career celebrity status, going to the ballpark, hitting the card shows, making appearances on TV and radio, as many ex-players do, Billy C. spent nearly a decade working with other members of the Conig clan to tend to the needs of a stricken family member who was incapable of taking care of himself.

"It was hard," Billy Conigliaro says now. "I don't think you ever get over something like that. It affected the entire family. But we were also a baseball family, and we have a lot of great memories."

In many ways, Billy C.'s career mirrored that of his older brother. Just as Tony C. was a young phenom from the Boston area who played for the hometown Red Sox, so, too, was Billy. Born in Revere, Massachusetts, on August 15, 1947, Billy Conigliaro grew up to become a high school baseball star. He was selected in the first round of the 1965 amateur draft by the Red Sox, and was just 21 years old when he made his major-league debut on April 11, 1969 as a pinch runner. With Tony playing right field that day, a 16-inning, 2-1 victory over the Cleveland Indians at Cleveland Municipal Stadium, it marked the first time the two brothers had appeared in a big-league game together.

Billy Conigliaro was traded to the Milwaukee Brewers at the end of the 1971 season and eventually landed with the Oakland A's, for whom he appeared in the 1973 League Championship Series and World Series. He had been slowed by a surgically repaired right knee but went to spring training in 1974 believing he had a chance to make the team. But despite a good spring, he was released a week before Opening Day, this because Oakland A's owner Charles O. Finley signed track star Herb Washington to be the club's "designated pinch runner."

Like his older brother, Billy C. attempted a comeback, this with the A's in 1976. He did not make the team. It was then that Billy Conigliaro put down his bat and picked up his camera, returning to Greater Boston.

Now, an older, wiser Billy Conigliaro, a witness to far too much tragedy, is ready to pick up a bat again. A fungo bat.

Where Have You Gone?

MIKE ANDREWS

It's rare for a retired big-league baseball player to look you square in the eye and put it out there that his greatest moments in life took place after he hung up the spikes. And admit it: If you did hear a player talk this kind of smack, you'd have a hard time believing it.

That is, unless it's former Red Sox second baseman Mike Andrews doing the talking. Understand, first, that this is a man who enjoyed a respectable eight-year career in the big leagues, most of it with the Red Sox. As a 24-year-old rookie, he was the second baseman on the 1967 "Impossible Dream" squad that won the American League pennant, and he went on to hit .308 in the World Series against the St. Louis Cardinals.

Yet it all seems so trivial when put up against what Mike Andrews has accomplished since he played his last big-league game. For nearly three decades Andrews has worked for the Jimmy Fund, the fundraising arm of the acclaimed Dana-Farber Cancer Institute, and when he speaks of "success stories," he speaks of children beating cancer, not throws beating runners.

The California native put in more than 20 years as executive director of the Jimmy Fund and remains its chairman. When he began, the

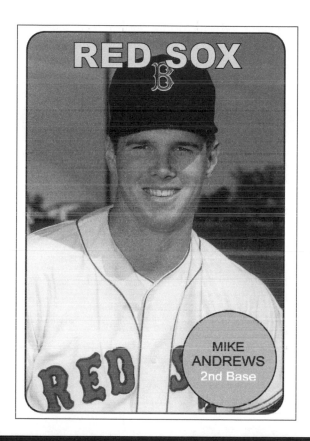

MIKE ANDREWS
Years with Red Sox: 1966-1970

Best Season with Red Sox: 1969

• Games: 121 • Batting Average: .293 • At Bats: 464 • Hits: 136 •
• Runs: 79 • Home Runs: 15 • RBIs: 59 • Slugging Percentage: .455 •

Jimmy Fund handled $800,000 in annual donations; in 2003, that number had climbed to $45 million.

"You can believe me or not believe me, but I've had many, many more thrills in my life after baseball than during baseball," he said. "This isn't to say I didn't have a lot of great days playing baseball, because I did. Just as I've had a lot of days with the Jimmy Fund that weren't so wonderful. That's going to happen when you lose kids to cancer. But I'll take the 26-plus years with the Jimmy Fund over the 13 years I had as a player."

Born in Los Angeles on July 9, 1943, Andrews signed with the Red Sox after graduating from South Torrance High School. He had a cup of coffee with the Red Sox late in the 1966 season, and by 1967 he settled in as the everyday second baseman for the "Impossible Dream" pennant winners.

During those early years in the big leagues, Andrews and his wife, Marilyn, whom he had dated in high school, would return home to California in the off-season.

"I was working for Sears," he said. "I was in the stock room. Don Buford, who played for the Orioles, was higher up on the ladder. He was out on the floor, in sporting goods. Well, I was taking home about $180 a week after taxes. But then we won the pennant in '67, and guys were calling me up and saying they were getting $300 for one appearance at a baseball banquet. That's all I had to hear. We moved to Boston."

As is the case with so many Red Sox players past and present, Andrews got involved in the Jimmy Fund as a volunteer, visiting kids in the hospital, signing autographs, doing whatever he could to help. As he put it, "Like everyone, I did my part, but not a whole lot more than other guys did."

It was Ken Coleman, the legendary radio and television voice of the Red Sox, who encouraged Andrews to increase his role. This was in the mid-'70s, after Andrews's playing career had ended and he was working in insurance at Mass Mutual. Coleman, active in the Jimmy Fund until the day he died in 2003, had left Boston for a few years to take a job in Cincinnati calling Reds games on television, but before leaving town he lined up Andrews to help run the Jimmy Fund in his absence.

"And I never left," he said. "When you see the progress being made every year in the fight against cancer, you realize how important the work is. We see success stories every day, and that's what makes it so rewarding to all of us."

Andrews's playing days with the Red Sox ended on December 1, 1970, when the team acquired shortstop Luis Aparicio from the Chicago White Sox for Andrews and infielder Luis Alvarado. Andrews spent most of the next three seasons with the White Sox but was picked up by the Oakland A's late in the '73 season after being released by the Chisox. It didn't hurt that Oakland's manager was Dick Williams, who had managed Andrews on the '67 Red Sox.

Andrews made the A's postseason roster, and then he made history. After making two errors in the 12th inning of Game 2 of the World Series, helping the New York Mets to a 10-7 victory, Charles O. Finley, the enraged owner of the A's, essentially fired Andrews, claiming the second baseman was injured. Finley hoped the "injury" would allow the A's to add young infielder Manny Trillo to the roster, but the scheme backfired when commissioner Bowie Kuhn ordered Andrews reinstated.

"After I was ordered back on the roster, Finley told Dick Williams not to play me under any circumstances," Andrews said. "Well, that's all Dick needed to hear."

Photo courtesy of Mike Andrews

Challenging Finley, Williams sent up Andrews to pinch hit for pitcher Horacio Pina in Game 4 at Shea Stadium.

"I don't know how you'd verify this, but I think I'm the only player in World Series history to get a standing ovation in the other team's park," said Andrews. "It was a special moment for me. And my teammates were great, too. When this all happened, they wore armbands with my number on them. But the thing is, it wasn't about me. This had been going on for a long time between Finley and the players. I guess this was the last straw."

At the conclusion of the 1973 World Series—the A's won it in seven games—Dick Williams handed in his resignation and resurfaced the next year as manager of the California Angels. As for Andrews, he was released by the A's less than a week after the World Series ended, his career over. But though he didn't know it at the time, his life's work was just beginning.

When he's not running the Jimmy Fund, Mike Andrews is one of the busiest family men in Boston. He and Marilyn have three children, all grown, and they now have six grandchildren—all girls—ranging in age from two to 21.

"Needless to say," said Andrews, "I'm busier now than I've ever been."

Where Have You Gone?

GARY WASLEWSKI

It was on a rainy night in Toledo that Gary Waslewski, a career minor-league pitcher, was told he was going to the big leagues.

Well . . . sort of.

Pitching for the Red Sox' Triple-A Toronto club in 1966, Waslewski and a collection of his teammates found themselves in the same bar as their fiery young manager, Dick Williams. The Maple Leafs' scheduled season opener against the Toledo Mud Hens had been rained out, and now, here they all were, a bunch of young players trading beers with their ambitious skipper, when, suddenly, the ambitious skipper made a brash promise.

"If we win the Governor's Cup championship this season, I'll be managing the Red Sox in 1967," Williams said. "And if you guys help me win the championship this year, I'll remember you guys next year."

Sure enough, the Toronto Maple Leafs went on to win their second consecutive Governor's Cup in 1966.

Sure enough, Dick Williams was named manager of the Red Sox for 1967.

And sure enough, Williams lobbied to bring several players—including such young players as Mike Andrews, Joe Foy and Reggie Smith—to the big leagues, along with a veteran minor-league catcher named

GARY WASLEWSKI
Years with Red Sox: 1967-1968

Best Season with Red Sox: 1968

• Games: 34 • Record: 4-7 • ERA: 3.67 • Innings Pitched: 105⅓ •
• Hits Allowed: 108 • Strikeouts: 59 • Walks: 40 • Saves: 2 •

Russ Gibson. And a veteran minor-league pitcher: 25-year-old righthander Gary Waslewski, who was beginning his eighth season of professional ball.

"Dick managed us to championships two years in a row, and in a lot of cases I was the guy he put on the mound against the teams we had to beat, which back then would have been Rochester and Richmond," he said. "Dick said I was a big-game pitcher. Little did I know, back then, what that would lead to."

What it led to, and to the surprise of many, was a chance to start Game 6 of the 1967 World Series for the Red Sox. The 100-to-1 long-shot Red Sox had shocked the baseball world by winning the American League pennant, but now, as Game 6 of the World Series loomed, they were trailing the St. Louis Cardinals three games to two.

"I was reading the papers that morning, and one guy wrote that Gary Waslewski has as much chance of winning as Custer had of beating the Indians," Waslewski said. "But it didn't bother me. I just went out and tried to do my job."

The way Waslewski saw it, he had already proved himself capable of pitching in the World Series, as he had worked three no-hit, no-run innings in Game 3, a 5-2 Boston loss.

"To me, that was the key," he said. "By the time I was starting Game 6, it was just like another game to me in the sense that I wasn't wowed by being in the World Series."

And that's the way he pitched. He allowed just two runs in five and one-third innings, leaving with a 4-2 lead. He lost his chance for a World Series victory when the Cardinals' Lou Brock tied the game with a two-run homer off John Wyatt, but the Red Sox went on to win the game, 8-4, tying the Series—thanks to Waslewski's solid outing.

A lifelong New Englander, Gary Lee Waslewski was born in Meriden, Connecticut, on July 21, 1941. A baseball and basketball star at Berlin High School, he attended the University of Connecticut for one year and then signed with the Pittsburgh Pirates. He was drafted by the Red Sox in 1965, but it was with the Maple Leafs in 1966 that he emerged as a "prospect," winning 18 games and earning International League Pitcher of the Year honors.

After all those years in the minors, the highlight of that thrilling '67 season for Waslewski was his June 15 start against the White Sox at Fenway Park. He worked nine shutout innings, allowing just six hits, yet the game remained deadlocked, as White Sox starter Bruce Howard and reliever Hoyt Wilhelm kept the Red Sox off the scoreboard.

The White Sox took a 1-0 lead in the top of the 11th on an RBI single by Ken Berry off reliever John Wyatt, but then the Red Sox won the game in the bottom of the 11th on a two-run homer by Tony Conigliaro.

"It was a no-decision for me, obviously, but it was my biggest thrill as a big-league pitcher to go out and pitch a game like that," Waslewski said. "And I think that was the game that got me to thinking we honestly had a chance to win the pennant. It set up what became a memorable summer for me."

Waslewski remained with the Red Sox through the 1968 season, but then lapsed into journeyman status. He pitched for the Cardinals, Expos, Yankees and Oakland A's over the next four seasons, making his last big-league appearance on September 28, 1972 for the A's, working two shutout innings for his old manager, Dick Williams.

After baseball, Waslewski and his wife, Nancy, whom he met while pitching in Toronto, settled down in Connecticut. They raised two sons —Dan, director of food and beverages at a Boston area country club, and Gary, an orthopedic surgeon in Scottsdale, Arizona. Gary and Nancy have five grandchildren.

Waslewski carved out a solid post-baseball career as a marketing rep for the Hartford Insurance Group. He specialized in estate planning, business insurance and pension plans, retiring in 1997.

He and his wife still make frequent drives from Connecticut to Fenway Park to take part in various team events. Waslewski garners little attention as he moves around the old yard, with most fans oblivious to the fact that this tall, slim, unassuming man delivered the goods in one of the most pressure-packed postseason games in franchise history.

Where Have You Gone?

RICO PETROCELLI

Tooling around in the Red Sox clubhouse one day before a game, Rico Petrocelli curled up with a good book—a book dealing with the principles of accounting.

Spotting the title of this weighty, businessy tome, Tony Conigliaro, perhaps Petrocelli's closest friend on the team, couldn't resist getting in some digs.

"What are you reading that stuff for?" Conigliaro asked, his tone suggesting he wasn't particularly interested in the answer.

"I'm planning for what I want do after my baseball career ends," said Petrocelli, trying to be serious.

"Then you should open a nightclub," said Conigliaro. "Or a lounge. Have some fun."

This exchange brilliantly captures the personalities of both men. Conigliaro, during his days with the Red Sox, was a notorious seeker of the nightlife in Boston and other cities, so, to him, it would have made sense to invest in some after-midnight haunt. And it also makes sense that Petrocelli, even when he was one of the game's best young players, would have been planning for life after baseball.

As things happened, Petrocelli never did follow his buddy's advice and go into the nightclub business. But he has done just about every-

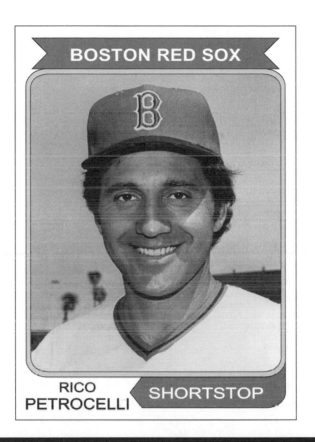

BOSTON RED SOX

RICO
PETROCELLI

SHORTSTOP

RICO PETROCELLI
Years with Red Sox: 1963-1976

Best Season with Red Sox: 1969

• Games: 154 • Batting Average: .297 • At Bats: 535 • Hits: 159 •
• Runs: 92 • Home Runs: 40 • RBIs: 97 • Slugging Percentage: .589 •

thing else. After his distinguished 13-year career ended following the 1976 season—his 210 career home runs still ranks him among the top 10 in club history—Petrocelli launched a variety of business ventures.

His latest effort is Petrocelli Marketing Group, located in Nashua, New Hampshire. The company handles projects ranging from promotional items and corporate gifts to golf accessories and logos, with Petrocelli, who turned 61 during the summer of 2004, running the show in concert with his son Mike.

As a player, did Petrocelli ever dream he'd live in a nine-to-five world? "Yeah, nine to five . . . that'll be the day," he said. "I'd love to have just one nine-to-five day. I'm very busy—and I'm very busy every day. But, really, I love it."

And it's all by design. Even as a minor-leaguer, the Brooklyn, New York-born Petrocelli was thinking about business. While with the Red Sox, he took accounting courses at two Boston area schools, Northeastern University and Bentley College. He hosted a sports talk show in 1977 and then served a year in the Red Sox broadcast booth with the late Ken Coleman, but he eventually opened a corporate cleaning business in the Boston area.

"But baseball wasn't out of my system," he said. "One day, I took a crew to this building we had to clean, and everything was going wrong, and then somebody handed me a message to call Ken Harrelson. That changed everything."

Hawk Harrleson, Petrocelli's one-time Red Sox teammate and a familiar presence in the team's television booth, had just been announced as the new general manager of the Chicago White Sox. Now, he was calling to offer Petrocelli a job as a minor-league manager.

"I told Hawk I'd have to think about it," Petrocelli said. "And then I said, 'Can you give me about 30 seconds?'"

Petrocelli quickly accepted the Hawk's offer. Then he got on the phone and consulted his wife, Elsie, who gave the plan her blessing. She was, after all, not unfamiliar with life in the minors: It was in the early 60s, while working at a Seattle restaurant called Keenohl's, across the street from Seattle's Sicks Stadium, that she met her future husband. Petrocelli was playing for the Triple-A Seattle Rainiers at the time.

Having signed on with the Hawk's White Sox, Petrocelli spent most of the next 10 years as a minor-league manager. Harrelson's tenure with the White Sox lasted just one year, but Petrocelli hung around for a few seasons before re-joining the Red Sox as a minor-league manager. In 1992, he managed Boston's Triple-A Pawtucket club.

Though he eventually returned to the business world, Petrocelli remained in the Boston area. And why not? He played his entire career in Boston, and he was a two-time All-Star shortstop before moving to third base late in his career. He hit 40 home runs in 1969, at the time an American-League record for home runs by a shortstop.

Petrocelli also made some local history: When the 100-to-1 longshot Red Sox clinched a tie for the American League pennant on the last day of the 1967 season, it was Petrocelli who caught a Rich Rollins pop-up for the final out. He gave the ball to teammate Jim Lonborg, the game's winning pitcher.

"But I still have the ball I hit for my 40th home run," he said. "It was off Jim Shellenback of the old Washington Senators, on the last night of the season in '69. At RFK Stadium. Somebody in the bullpen got the ball for me, and I have it on a shelf at home. That home run is one of the great personal memories of my career."

But not all of the memories are sweet. In the fourth inning of an August 18, 1967 game against the California Angels, Petrocelli was on deck when his buddy, Tony Conigliaro, was hit in the left eye by a pitch from the Angels' Jack Hamilton. Conigliaro missed the remainder of the season, and, though he made a couple of dramatic comebacks, was never the same again.

"I can still hear the sound of that pitch hitting him," Petrocelli said. "It was terrible, like a melon exploding. And when I leaned over him, I could see his whole face blow up. It was just about the worst moment of my life."

Petrocelli went on to hit two home runs in the '67 World Series against the St. Louis Cardinals. Eight years later, he and Carl Yastrzemski were the only veterans of the '67 squad to face the Cincinnati Reds in the 1975 World Series, with Petrocelli hitting .308 in the seven-game series against the victorious Big Red Machine.

"But it's the '67 season people talk about," Petrocelli said. "Not a week goes by without somebody mentioning it. It changed baseball forever in New England, and I'm glad I played a part in it."

Where Have You Gone?

DICK RADATZ

During an era in which the big-league bullpen was used mostly as a dumping ground for baseball's old, hopeless hasbeens and young, hopeful maybes, Dick Radatz was a breed unto himself. One of the first pitchers trained to be a relief specialist, the man known as The Monster made 381 appearances during his seven years in the big leagues—and not one of them was as a starter.

He was, and to this day remains, a mountain of a man. Listed as six foot six, 230 pounds during his playing days, Radatz appeared ever more menacing when standing on the mound, and he was a Monster without mystery: When stepping up to the plate to face Radatz, opposing hitters knew they were going to be treated to fastballs, fastballs and more fastballs. And most of those hitters knew they were going to fail: From his rookie year in 1962 through 1965, Radatz saved exactly 100 games for the Red Sox, and four more in 1966 before being shipped off to the Cleveland Indians.

"That had to be the worst time of my life," said Radatz, who eventually settled in the Boston area after his playing career ended. "It wasn't that I was going to Cleveland, it was that I was coming from Boston. We had bad teams back then, but I loved the city. I loved everything about it."

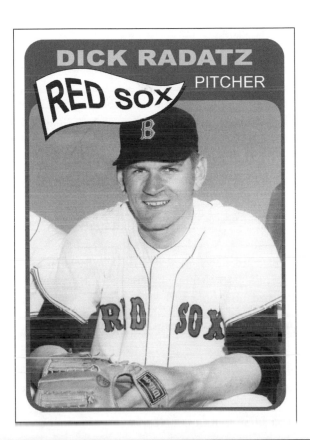

DICK RADATZ
Years with Red Sox: 1962-1966

Best Season with Red Sox: 1964

• Games: 79 • Record: 16-9 • ERA: 2.29 • Innings Pitched: 124⅓ •
• Hits Allowed: 103 • Strikeouts: 181 • Walks: 58 • Saves: 29 •

It's true: The Red Sox were terrible during the Monster's four full seasons in Boston, finishing no higher than seventh in the 10-team American League, averaging about 89 losses a season during this period—and often playing to sparse crowds at Fenway Park, unless the Yankees were in town.

But Radatz always gave 'em a thrill. Not limiting his relief appearances to the modern-day one inning, Radatz often worked two or three innings out of the bullpen. Incredibly, he won 15 games in 1963 and 16 in '64—again, all in relief. At a time when the team was going nowhere in the standings, fans would hang around for the trademark Radatz finish: When the Monster had secured the game's final out, usually by strikeout, he would thrust both arms high into the air, the hardball equivalent of King Kong atop the Empire State Building.

Mickey Mantle, the slugging icon of the era, and a star with the Yankees, was virtually inept against Radatz. In 63 career at-bats against Radatz, Mantle struck out 47 times. He had just one career hit against Radatz, a home run to right field on June 17, 1964.

"It was at Yankee Stadium," Radatz said. "He thought he had popped it up, so he threw his bat a good 30 feet in disgust. But the ball kept going, and it left the park. Mantle had had all kind of problems with me over the years, and now he was swearing at me all the way around the bases. It was a lot of take-that-you-no-good-son-of-a-bitch stuff."

"Mickey was a switch hitter, and of course batted left-handed against me," Radatz said. "My plan was to always work him inside and get ahead on the count, and then go up the ladder with him. And he always bit. He got so frustrated that he even tried to bunt off me a couple of times. Years later, I asked him if he ever thought about hitting right-handed off me. I was just kidding, but he got all serious and said, 'I actually thought about doing that.'"

According to Radatz, his never-to-be-forgotten nickname—The Monster—was coined by Mantle.

"But he had an adjective before it," said Radatz.

His fastball having diminished after his years in Boston, Radatz drifted from the Indians to the Cubs to the Tigers, winding up his career with the Montreal Expos in 1970. The Michigan native—and proud alum of Michigan State—returned home after his playing days, but eventually drifted back to Boston, where he discovered he was just as popular as he had been during his days in the Sox' bullpen.

He worked in television and radio, as well as in a variety of business ventures. He also took a turn at the typewriter, authoring a collection of youth baseball coaching manuals. To this day, youth baseball remains a red-button topic for Radatz.

"Kids give up baseball at 13 because they haven't been taught how to play the game properly," Radatz said. "They have coaches who tell them one thing, and then they get in the car and their fathers are all saying, 'Don't pay any attention to him. He doesn't know what he's talking about.' By the time they're done with Little League and ready for Babe Ruth baseball, a lot of them give up and go find something else to do, such as watch television or play video games."

On sports talk radio in Boston, the old-timey Radatz became a critic of modern-day "pitch counts," and of pitching coaches who don't place enough emphasis on what be believes is a moundsmen's ultimate weapon, the fastball.

"I've never understood the whole pitch count thing," Radatz said. "The more you throw, the stronger your arm gets. That's a given, provided you have a decent arm to begin with."

Years earlier, the Monster's son, Dick Radatz Jr., carved out a career as a minor-league executive. At one point he was the general manager of the Red Sox' Winter Haven club in the Single-A Florida State League. And then, in 2003, as he turned 66, the Monster himself took a turn at minor-league baseball, traveling to nearby Lynn, Massachusetts, to become pitching coach of the North Shore Spirit, who play in the independent Northeast League.

"Yes, we do have pitch counts," said Radatz, in response to the inevitable question. "But we don't automatically yank a guy after 80, 90, or 100 pitches. If he's doing OK, we just leave him alone. That's the way it should be."

DAVE STAPLETON

On the night the Red Sox were completing their four-game sweep of the St. Louis Cardinals to win their first World Series championship in 86 years, Dave and Cheryl Stapleton were driving to Birmingham, Alabama, from their home in Daphne, down south on the Mobile Bay, to attend a volleyball tournament in which their daughter was participating.

When they arrived at the AmeriSuites in Birmingham, they quickly did the front-desk check-in thing and made way for their room, wanting to make sure they could see the end of the game. For the Stapletons were, and are, Red Sox fans—Cheryl had been indoctrinated in Red Sox fandom while growing up in Seekonk, Massachusetts, and it so happened that she fell in love and married a man who would play seven seasons with the Red Sox. And their kids naturally became Red Sox fans, so much so that Shaun, the oldest, had made a promise to his classmates at Auburn University that he'd shave his head if the Red Sox won the World Series.

Now, back to that hotel room. Dave and Cheryl threw down their suitcases and turned on the television, and guess what? With the Red Sox closing in on their clinching victory over the Cardinals in Game 4 of the World Series, they had made a number of late-game, leave-nothing-to-

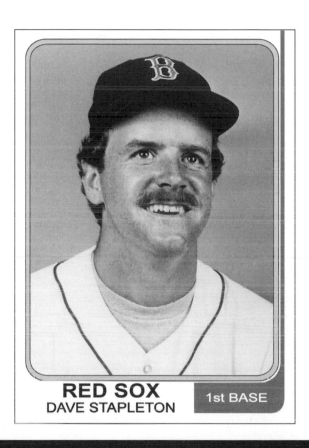

RED SOX
DAVE STAPLETON

1st BASE

DAVE STAPLETON
Years with Red Sox: 1980-1986

Best Season with Red Sox: 1980

• Games: 106 • Batting Average: .321 • At Bats: 449 • Hits: 144 •
• Runs: 61 • Home Runs: 7 • RBIs: 45 • Slugging Percentage: .463 •

chance defensive changes, including this one: Doug Mientkiewicz, a top-rate glove man, had gone in to play first base in place of David Ortiz.

And it got Dave Stapleton to wondering: Had the Red Sox made that kind of change in Game 6 of the 1986 World Series against the New York Mets—with Stapleton replacing Bill Buckner—this so-called curse nonsense would have been eradicated 18 years earlier.

"I guess I'll always wonder about that one," said Stapleton, now the owner of a residential construction business in his native Alabama. "I don't know if Buckner went up to (manager) John McNamara and said he wanted to stay in the game, or if McNamara did it on his own. What I do know is that McNamara was afraid of the veteran players, guys like Buckner and (Jim) Rice, so I guess that's why I didn't go in."

Even youthful baseball fans not yet alive in 1986 know well this terrible chapter in Red Sox history. With Game 6 tied 3-3 after nine innings, the Sox scored two runs in the top of the 10th to take a 5-3 lead, leaving this long-tortured franchise just three outs away from capturing its first World Series since 1918.

Logic—and recent history—dictated that McNamara would remove the hobbled Buckner from the game in the bottom of the 10th inning in favor of Stapleton, a better defensive player at this point of Buckner's career. In every game the Red Sox had won during the 1986 postseason—Games 2, 5, 6 and 7 of the American League Championship Series against the California Angels and Games 1, 2 and 5 of the World Series against the Mets—McNamara had made the late-inning Buckner-Stapleton switch.

Yet now, with the Red Sox on the cusp of winning the World Series, Buckner remained at first base. The Mets rallied for three runs to win the game, the deciding run coming across when Mookie Wilson's dribbler down the first-base line went infamously between Buckner's legs. The Mets went on to capture the World Series with an 8-5 victory over the Red Sox in Game 7.

"You wonder how history might have been different had McNamara made that change," said Stapleton. "I later heard him make some kind of reference about me being 'shaky' at first base, which is pretty funny. If I was so shaky, why did he put me out there in all those other games? And I didn't look 'shaky' in the ninth inning of Game 1, when I picked up a bunt by Ray Knight and forced the runner at second."

Game 6 of the 1986 World Series has been one of the most written about and debated moments in baseball history, but most of the discussion has focused on Buckner, who made the historic error, rather than Stapleton, who should have been playing first base in the 10th inning. The assumption has always been that McNamara, in a nod to his beloved veterans, wanted Buckner on the field for the grand celebration.

Stapleton not only didn't get into Game 6, he never again appeared in the big leagues. Having just finished his seventh season with the Red Sox, Stapleton was granted free agency in November of 1986, and, seeking a team that might offer him more playing time, he signed with the Seattle Mariners. He thought he had locked up a spot on the Mariners' Opening Day roster in '87, only to be released the last day of spring training.

"They called me in June of that year and told me they needed some help in the minor leagues," he said. "They asked me if I would go to Double-A and play first base, the idea being that they'd see what happened after that. But I was home by then, and I decided maybe it was time I spent more time with my family. And that's what I've been doing ever since."

Stapleton partnered with an old friend in a construction business, and eventually founded his own company. He and Cheryl, a former New England Patriots cheerleader, have three children: the noggin-shaved Shaun; Joshua, who followed in his dad's footsteps by accepting a baseball scholarship at the University of South Alabama (he's a left-handed-hitting second baseman) and Cara, who in the fall of 2004 was still a senior in high school—and dragging her parents all across Alabama for volleyball tournaments.

For Dave Stapleton, who was born in Fairhope, Alabama, in 1954, living in nearby Daphne is nothing dramatic. But what about Cheryl Stapleton, a New England girl and lifelong Red Sox/Patriots fan?

"I've been down here for so long that this is home," she said, speaking with the slight southern accent she's acquired over the years. "But we have this house filled with Red Sox fans, so in a lot of ways it feels like Boston."

Where Have You Gone?

JERRY MOSES

Author's Note: Though he was named Gerald Braheen Moses at birth and his shortened first name is often spelled as "Gerry," the former Red Sox catcher prefers "Jerry," and so is referred to as such in this chapter.

Jerry Moses will always be identified as a member of the Red Sox. Born in Yazoo City, Mississippi, on August 9, 1946, Moses signed his first professional contract with the Sox, and one year later, in 1965, he was just 18 years old when he registered his first big-league at-bat—with the Red Sox. And though Moses would eventually become a catching vagabond, logging time with six different teams after leaving Boston, he spent parts of four seasons with the Red Sox, including a selection to the 1970 All-Star Game.

Yet on August 1, 1973, when the Red Sox had one of their most infamous dust-ups with the Yankees, their long-time rivals from the Bronx, Moses found himself in the opposite dugout, working for the team in the gray road uniforms.

First, the specifics: In the top of the ninth inning of a Wednesday afternoon game between the Red Sox and Yankees on August 1, 1973 at Fenway Park, the game tied 2-2, Yankees catcher Thurman Munson doubled to left and advanced to third on a grounder to second. After

JERRY MOSES
Years with Red Sox: 1965-1970

Best Season with Red Sox: 1969

• Games: 53 • Batting Average: .304 • At Bats: 135 • Hits: 41 •
• Runs: 13 • Home Runs: 4 • RBIs: 17 • Slugging Percentage: .474 •

Felipe Alou was walked intentionally, the next batter, Gene Michael, attempted to drop a bunt on a squeeze play as Munson charged down the line. He missed. Fisk then slammed down a tag on Munson, and in the process dumped the burly Yankee catcher on his head. The two men were soon throwing haymakers, the benches emptied, and, when peace was restored, both Fisk and Munson were ejected.

And running in from the bullpen to take Munson's place behind the plate in the bottom of the ninth was Jerry Moses.

Looking back on that game, Moses said, "By the time I ran in from the bullpen, the fight was over. So I missed it."

But Moses has an interesting theory about the Munson-Fisk fight.

"I've never really said this before, but I've always wondered if Stick (Michael) and Munson may have had that play set up before it happened," he said. "Michael was always a pretty level-headed guy, a smart player, which is why he's been successful as a baseball executive, but Munson was a heady, emotional guy. And he just hated Fisk. They hated each other. They were the same type of player—tough, aggressive—and there was a rivalry there. So it makes me wonder what was going on that day."

What we do know is this: The modern Red Sox-Yankees rivalry, dormant for many years, was rekindled that day. But Moses, who remains a regular visitor to Fenway Park, was a Yankee that day.

"Don't get me wrong, I enjoyed playing with the Yankees very much," he said. "But I would have been very happy had I never left the Red Sox."

Summoned to the big leagues for a brief fill-in role in 1965, Moses immediately opened eyes. In a May 25 game against the Minnesota Twins, Moses pinch hit for pitcher Bob Heffner and slammed a home run. At 18 years, nine months old, he became the youngest player in history to hit a pinch-hit home run, taking Mudcat Grant out of the park.

It wasn't until 1968 that Moses returned to the big leagues, and not until a year later that he received any appreciable playing time. He got off to a fast start in 1970 and was named to the American League All-Star squad, but did not get into the game. (The game featured one of the most memorable endings in All-Star history, with Pete Rose barreling into Ray Fosse with the winning run. Had Rose been out, it would have been Moses going into the game for the injured Fosse.)

Moses never matched his 1970 All-Star form. Traded to the Angels at the end of the season, he spent the rest of his career bouncing around from the Angels to the Indians to the Yankees to the Tigers to the Padres to the White Sox, never spending more than a season with any one team.

"What I lacked," Moses said, "was confidence in myself. I worked really hard, as hard as anyone, but looking back on it I think I doubted myself. Most catchers have more or less the same amount of talent, and it's confidence that takes some of them to a higher level."

That's the bad news.

The good news?

"Thank God for second careers," said Moses. "Whatever confidence I may have lacked in baseball, I didn't lack confidence once I left baseball. Or maybe I just learned from my experience as a baseball player."

In his career after baseball, Moses has been a spectacularly successful businessman. He had already been working for Ogden Food Services before his playing days ended, and he eventually branched out and started his own business, Fanfare, which provided concessions for arenas, stadiums, conventions and amphitheaters. He sold the business to Fine Host in 1993, and since then has worked in a variety of business ventures. He opened a commercial bakery business with his son, Steve, a former minor-league baseball player, with Red Sox legend Carl Yastrzemski on board as a partner. Moses also does work with Boston Culinary, owned by Boston businessman Joe O'Donnell, who tried unsuccessfully to purchase the Red Sox in 2001.

Why has Moses been so successful as a businessman?

"I believe luck is a good place to begin," he said. "But luck can only take you so far. It also requires building relationships and knowing how to work with people. If you don't know how to sell yourself and your product, you're not going to go very far."

Moses and his wife, Carolyn, continue to live in the Boston area, as do their two children, Steve and Kristin. They have four grandchildren.

And, yes, Moses was rooting for the Red Sox to take down the Yankees in the 2004 American League Championship Series.

"And when the Red Sox won the World Series, it was the greatest thing in the world," he said. "I'll always see myself as a member of the Red Sox. You don't lose that. It was a great day for us."

EARL WILSON

Most of the big automobile assembly lines in and around Detroit were shut down for the holidays, and so, too, was a smaller company called Autotek Sealants, which provides sound-deadening material for new cars.

But when a call was placed to Autotek on the day before New Year's Eve, 2004, it was the owner of the company who picked up the phone.

"Well, it's what I do—work," said former Red Sox pitcher Earl Wilson, who started the company with his wife, Roslin. "You know, I'm not exactly Phi Beta Kappa, but I'm not afraid to work. And that's all you need—a willingness to work. That, and people taking a liking to you."

Wilson, who played three seasons with the Tigers after being ridiculously traded by the Red Sox, settled in the Detroit area after his playing career ended. He was working in sales for a while, but it occurred to him one day that he could do a better job running a company than the people who were signing his paychecks.

And so it was that Autotek was born.

"Well, Roslin basically runs the place," said Wilson. "She does all the inside work and I'm always on the outside, trying to drum up new busi-

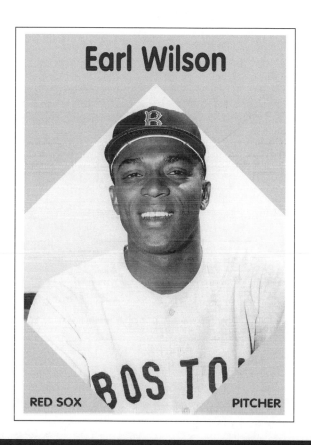

Earl Wilson

RED SOX   PITCHER

EARL WILSON
Years with Red Sox: 1959-1966

Best Season with Red Sox: 1962

• Games: 31 • W-L Record: 12-8 • ERA: 3.90 • Innings Pitched: 191⅓ •
• Hits Allowed: 163 • Strikeouts: 137 • Walks: 111 • Complete Games: 4 •

ness. I guess now the job has a fancy title, sales executive or something like that. But what I really am is a peddler."

Had the Red Sox been a bit more level-headed in the 1960s, Earl Wilson might be doing his peddling in the Boston area this very day. Promoted to the big leagues in 1959—just a few weeks after Pumpsie Green, thus making him the *second* African-American to play for the Red Sox—Wilson soon became one of the best pitchers on some truly bad teams. He threw a no-hitter against the Los Angeles Angels in 1962, his first full year in the big leagues, ending the season with a 12-8 record.

But Wilson was never one to keep his mouth zipped when he felt threatened or slighted, and this was particularly true in matters of race.

He remembers a day when Red Sox players were asked to line up to have their pictures taken. He says that when he stepped in front of the camera, Bucky Harris, who was general manager of the Red Sox in 1959 and '60, was heard to remark that "that's wasted film."

He remembers the year the Red Sox moved their spring training facility from Scottsdale, Arizona, to Winter Haven, Florida. Wilson was asked if black players would have any "problems" in Winter Haven, and he was told, no, there'd be no trouble.

"They said they checked it out," Wilson said. "They said, 'Go anywhere you want, do anything you want.' Well, I went to a little bar one day with Dick Radatz and a couple of guys, and I was denied the privilege of entering the place.

"When I went back to the ballpark the next day, I was told not to say anything about it because it might hurt my career. I said, 'Man, I don't have a career, and I'm not going to let that stop me from being a man by exposing it. 'Well, later that year I was traded from Boston to Detroit."

Radatz confirms the story.

"It was Earl, myself and Dave Morehead," he said. "We all asked for Budweisers, and this redneck guy behind the bar said, 'I'll serve you two guys, but not the nigger.'"

Looking back on the incident, and the eventual trade that landed him in Detroit in exchange for outfielder Dom Demeter (who played parts of two seasons with the Red Sox) and pitcher Julio Navarro (who never made a big-league appearance with the Sox), Wilson is philosophical. He went on to have his best years with the Tigers—including a 22-11 record in 1967—and he soon acquired a lot of friends in Detroit, a city he found to be more racially tolerant than Boston.

"Ninety-nine percent of the people I met in Boston were great to me," he said. "But it was a city with problems. It's still a city with problems. But I believe progress is being made.

"When I broke in, there were some bad guys," Wilson said. "Harris was a bad guy, and he was friends with Mike Higgins, the manager, and he was a bad guy, too.

"But I don't think it's like that with the Red Sox any more," he said. "I've met Lou Gorman, and he's one of the nicest people. And I met the new owners a few years ago when I came to Boston to attend a banquet. They strike me as quality people."

Born in Ponchatoula, Louisiana, on October 2, 1934, Wilson signed with the Red Sox after a brief stay at San Diego State. He was a catcher at the time. But while playing for the Bisbee-Douglas Copper Kings of the Arizona-Texas League in 1953, he was converted into a pitcher by his manager, Syd Cohen, himself a pitcher in the 1930s with the old Washington Senators.

"The only reason they did that was because they didn't have any pitching," said Wilson. "Cohen said to me, 'Can you pitch?' so I went out and pitched. And I was a pitcher from that point on."

One would think Wilson is thankful for the switch, given that he went on to an 11-year career in the big leagues, winning 121 games. But he has a different take, pointing out that his hitting talents would also have taken him to the big leagues had he remained a catcher.

The man has a point. For Earl Wilson was one of baseball's best-hitting pitchers during his years in the big leagues. He had a career .195 average, pretty good for a pitcher, and he believes that number would have been much higher had he been getting three or four at-bats every day. He also hit 35 career home runs, including two seasons with seven homers, and understand that we're talking about some serious smashes here, balls that sailed deep into the bleachers and beyond.

Wilson has also been involved with the Baseball Assistance Team (B.A.T.), a non-profit wing of Major League Baseball that provides financial assistance to baseball players in times of trouble, serving as president and CEO.

He has three sons, Greg, Marvin and Mark, from an earlier marriage.

Where Have You Gone?

BOBBY DOERR

On Saturday, October 16, 2004, the Red Sox invited three of their oldest, best and most-beloved ex-players—Bobby Doerr, Dom DiMaggio and Johnny Pesky—to throw out the first pitch for Game 3 of the American League Championship Series against the New York Yankees.

And what a great moment it was to see those three players, all of them participants in the 1946 World Series, walk out to the Fenway mound, baseballs in hand. But it was the high point of the evening for the packed Fenway house, as the Red Sox went out and dropped a humiliating 19-8 decision to the Yankees, leaving the Sox on the brink of elimination.

But as the old ballpark emptied out, Sox fans bracing for yet another winter of second-guessing and ruing over what might have been, at least one man connected with the Red Sox didn't seem too upset.

And that man was one of the three first-pitch tossers, Hall of Famer Bobby Doerr.

On his way out of a private box after the Sox' lopsided loss, Doerr bumped into team president Larry Lucchino.

"I'll see you at the World Series," Doerr said.

"What's that?" asked Lucchino.

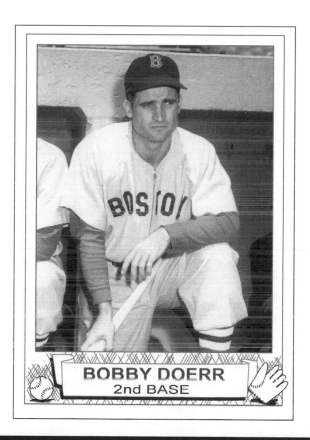

BOBBY DOERR
2nd BASE

BOBBY DOERR
Years with Red Sox: 1937-1951

Best Season with Red Sox: 1950

• Games: 149 • Batting Average: .294 • At Bats: 586 • Hits: 172 •
• Runs: 103 • Home Runs: 27 • RBIs: 120 • Slugging Percentage: .519 •

"You heard me," Doerr said. "The World Series. I'll be back next week."

And so it came to pass. The Red Sox rebounded with four straight victories to eliminate their storied rivals from New York, and then swept the St. Louis Cardinals for their first World Series championship since 1918. But just as the comeback speaks volumes about the strength, resolve and optimism of the 2004 Red Sox, it also speaks volumes about the strength, resolve and optimism of Robert Pershing Doerr, who, in addition to being a Hall of Fame second baseman, also happens to be the owner of a Hall of Fame disposition.

"I guess I was always that way," said Doerr, a grandfather and great-grandfather who splits his time between his ranch in Junction City, Oregon, and a home off the Rogue River in Agness, Oregon. "I've always been a believer in not letting things get you down. I believe I've always been very lucky in that I understood how important it is to be positive and to surround yourself with good friends."

It was that attitude toward life that resulted in Doerr being the unofficial captain of those great Red Sox teams of the 1940s, including the 1946 American League pennant winners who went down to defeat in Game 7 of the World Series against the St. Louis Cardinals. And while that Series forever remained a thorny issue with Sox legend Ted Williams, who was injured and hit just .200 against the Cardinals, it was a crowning achievement for Doerr, who hit .409, including a two-run home run off Cardinals pitcher Red Munger in Game 4.

But Doerr was never a seeker of the spotlight, and he was, and remains, a defender of Ted Williams. Doerr also has some thoughts on what the Red Sox might have done to help Williams in his seemingly never-ending battles with fans and the media.

"They should have gotten counseling for him," said Doerr. "The man was under so much pressure, and everyone wanted a piece of him—the writers, the fans, everyone. And it used to eat at him, and a lot of times he was unhappy.

"If they had worked with him, and gotten someone for him to talk to, and, as I said, if they had gotten him some counseling now and then, I think Ted would have been a lot more comfortable. He was a good man who just needed that little extra help."

Is it any wonder this man was considered the captain of the Red Sox? Born on April 7, 1918, Doerr was playing for the San Diego Padres in the Pacific Coast League when he was signed by the Red Sox. It was a truly historic train ride to the west coast for Sox general manager Eddie Collins, who came away with two future Hall of Famers: Williams and Doerr.

Doerr had just turned 19 when he made his major-league debut with the Red Sox on April 20, 1937, collecting three hits in an 11-5 victory over the Philadelphia Athletics.

But perhaps more importantly to Doerr was the debut he was making in Oregon. Like Williams, Doerr was an avid outdoorsman and fisherman, and he had fallen in love with Oregon while playing in the Pacific Coast League. He visited the area during the off season, and so happened to meet a woman from South Dakota who was teaching in a one-room schoolhouse. The woman's name was Monica, and, as Doerr put it, "She had no interest in me as a ballplayer. She didn't know a baseball from a football, but that was just fine with me."

They were married in 1938, and remained "best friends" until December, 2003, when Monica, who had suffered a series of strokes, passed away. But while Doerr clearly misses Monica—and anyone who saw them in recent years couldn't help but notice how the old ballplayer doted on his ailing wife— he remains upbeat and active, often getting out of the house in the morning to chop wood.

Doerr's playing career ended before the start of the 1952 season because of a chronically ailing back. He returned to Oregon and bought a ranch, and in 1957 he took a job as a minor-league coach with the Red Sox. In 1965, the Sox named him a coach of their Triple-A Toronto farm club, where he teamed up with brash, young manager Dick Williams. The Maple Leafs won back-to-back International League championships in '65 and '66, after which Williams was named manager of the Red Sox. He took Doerr along as his first-base coach, making Doerr the only man in uniform to be involved with Boston's 1946 and 1967 pennant-winning teams.

Williams was fired as manager in the last days of the 1969 season, after which Doerr returned home to Oregon, believing his baseball days were over. But he had apparently made an impression during his two seasons coaching the minor-league Maple Leafs; when major-league baseball arrived in Toronto in 1977, Doerr was added to the staff as hitting coach. He remained with the team for five seasons, retiring in 1981.

Doerr received baseball's highest honor in 1986, when he and Monica made the trip to Cooperstown, New York, for his Hall of Fame enshrinement. On May 24, 1988, Doerr's uniform No. 1 was retired by the Red Sox.

Where Have You Gone?

FRANK MALZONE

The hallway that leads from the elevator to the Fenway Park pressbox is smartly adorned with framed black-and-white photographs of some of the hardball greats whose talents were often on display—for real, rather than on film—in this old ballyard.

There's a nice picture of Tris Speaker, Duffy Lewis and Harry Hooper, the outfield trio who powered the 1912 Red Sox to a World Series title. Over there, there's Teddy Ballgame. To the left, Lefty Grove. And then there's the picture that for many years has caught both my gaze and my curiosity: It shows a smiling Frank Malzone, who played third base for the Red Sox from 1955 to 1965, being presented a beautiful new Thunderbird convertible. And behind man and car is a banner, on which are printed the words: "Congratulations to the nicest guy in baseball."

And I've always wondered: Just what does a guy have to do to be proclaimed the nicest guy in baseball?

And, yes, I've also wondered: Whatever became of that crisp, new Thunderbird convertible?

"Well, I have no idea why they decided to give me the car or why they thought I was such a nice guy," said Malzone. "A couple of fans came up to me one day and said they wanted to set up a day for me, and

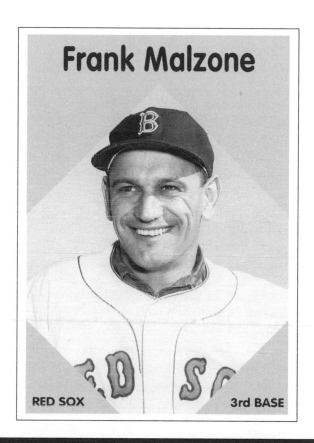

Frank Malzone

RED SOX   3rd BASE

FRANK MALZONE
Years with Red Sox: 1955-1965

Best Season with Red Sox: 1962

• Games: 156 • Batting Average: .283 • At Bats: 619 • Hits: 175 •
• Runs: 74 • Home Runs: 21 • RBIs: 95 • Slugging Percentage: .426 •

I was flattered, of course, but I told them I didn't have any control over those things.

"So they went to the club, and the club thought it was a great idea, and so they had this big day for me. It was in 1960. It was a little embarrassing, but a lot of fun."

And the car?

"Rode like a dream," he said. "We had it for five or six years. But then I stopped playing, and we had five kids to raise, and I needed the money. So I figured we'd keep the station wagon and sell the Thunderbird. I took it down to the gas station and this guy there sold it for me. I don't know what happened to it after that. I wish I still had it. It's probably worth a lot of money now."

Even Frank's wife, Amy, misses that great ride.

"It was one of those cars with all the push buttons," she said. "You'd just press a button and the roof would come up and disappear into the back. It wasn't like those old cars, where you had to get out and do all the work. What a great car."

What a great couple. Frank and Amy—"I call her by her real name, Amelia, when I'm mad at her," said Frank—settled in the Boston area after Malzone's career ended. There, they raised their five kids, including John, himself an infielder who played in the minor leagues and got as high as Triple-A. Today the Malzones have six grandchildren and two great-grandchildren.

Born in the Bronx, New York, on February 28, 1930, Malzone made his big-league debut with the Red Sox in the last days of the 1955 season, appearing in six games, including a six-for-10 performance in a doubleheader against the Baltimore Orioles. He appeared in 27 games in 1956 and then made the team for good in '57, becoming a fixture at third base for most of the next decade.

He had played with the Red Sox from 1955 through the 1965 season, during which he was one of the game's best-fielding third basemen, winning three consecutive Gold Gloves (until Brooks Robinson came along and owned the award the next 16 seasons) and then put in a year with the California Angels before calling it quits. Looking for work, he called the Red Sox, who thought it would be a good idea to bring "the nicest guy in baseball" back into the fold. They hired him as an amateur scout, and then let him loose on the ballfields of New England in search of raw talent.

But in the last months of the 1967 season, the Sox sent Malzone outside New England, asking him to scout the Minnesota Twins, who would close out the season with a series against the Red Sox at Fenway Park.

"I followed the Twins for about 10 days, and then I came back to Fenway and there was this big meeting," he said. "They were all there—Tom Yawkey, (general manager) Dick O'Connell, (manager) Dick Williams. I didn't even have any notes. Had it all in my head. They asked me what I thought of the Twins, and the only thing I remember saying is, 'Don't let Harmon Killebrew beat you.' That was it.

"Well, we beat the Twins and won the pennant, and next thing I knew I was the advance scout."

He would spend the next 27 years advancing for the Red Sox, earning a reputation as one of the best scouts in the business. He survived era after era, new regime after new regime, and in the 90s he took on a new role as the team's National League evaluator.

"I still work for the club," said Malzone, who turned 75 during spring training of 2005. "I do some consulting here and there. I'll work with the kids in Pawtucket and Portland during the season, and I also go to spring training."

Malzone was particularly thrilled in October, 2004, when the Red Sox won their first World Series in 86 years.

"That was the only thing I missed as a player—we never won anything," he said. "We had some good teams when I first came up, when we had Ted Williams, Jimmy Piersall, Jackie Jensen and those guys, but it was always the same thing every year: You'd play as hard as you could, but in the end the Yankees would go to the World Series and we'd go home.

"That's why 2004 was so much fun," he said. "Except for that one season with the Angels, I've been with the Red Sox for 50 years. It was nice to see the Red Sox send the Yankees home for once."

Where Have You Gone?

SAM HORN

W hen Sam Horn's playing career ended, the man once known to Red Sox fans as the Fenway Fridge returned to New England and settled in Rhode Island. He had been a fan favorite in Boston, but he was also something of a legend in Rhode Island, where, during his days with the Sox' Triple-A Pawtucket club, he hit tape-measure home runs about which the locals continue to buzz.

But once he and his wife, Debra, had found a place in Rhode Island, the next question became: What's the big guy going to do with the rest of his life?

"My first thought," said Horn, who was born and raised in San Diego, "was that I wanted to be a coach. I wanted to be a hitting coach. I may not have been the best hitter in baseball history, but I do know *how* to hit, and I always thought I could be a good teacher."

Armed with this confidence in his own abilities to educate eager minor-leaguers on the finer points of hitting, Sam Horn got on the phone one morning and placed a call to the Red Sox. He told them he was living in the area, that he was looking for work in baseball, that he'd like to talk with the club about any openings they might have.

Sure, the Red Sox said, come on up to Boston, let's talk.

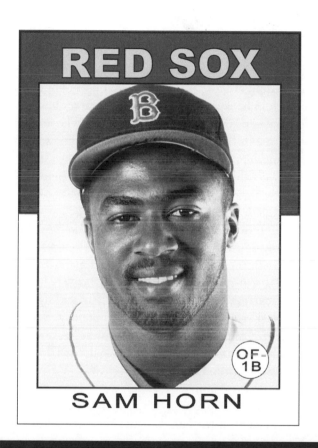

RED SOX

OF-1B

SAM HORN

SAM HORN
Years with Red Sox: 1987-1989

Best Season with Red Sox: 1987

• Games: 46 • Batting Average: .278 • At Bats: 158 • Hits: 44 •
• Runs: 31 • Home Runs: 14 • RBIs: 34 • Slugging Percentage: .589 •

"So I drove up to Fenway Park from Rhode Island, and I met a lot of people," Horn said. "We talked about a lot of things. We talked about baseball, and my philosophy about baseball, things like that. And then I went home, hoping they'd call me."

And the Red Sox *did* call, only it was with an invitation to try something Horn had never considered: Television. With the Red Sox and their cable television arm, NESN, now under the direction of new ownership, a decision had been made to spruce up the network's pre- and postgame shows, and the idea was that Horn, hugely popular during his playing days, would be equally popular in front of a camera.

"They had me come back for what was basically an audition," Horn said. "They put me in front of a camera and asked me some questions. Then they had me come back a second time. Then they tried it with me wearing a suit. Next thing you know, they're offering me a job to work in television."

Horn had exploded into popularity as a Red Sox player practically from the day he arrived in the big leagues. Called up from Triple-A Pawtucket on July 23, 1987, this after he had belted 30 home runs in just 333 at-bats with the Pawsox, Horn made his major-league debut on July 25 and hit a two-run homer off Seattle Mariners lefthander Stan Clarke. The next day he had three more hits, including a home run. Through his first six games in the big leagues, the 6-5, 240-pound outfielder/first baseman had four home runs. By the time the season was over, he had 14 home runs in 158 at-bats. Toss in his Triple-A numbers, and that's 44 home runs in 491 at-bats.

"That was an exciting summer for me," said Horn, who then lapsed into a little third-person discourse, as the man often does: "Sam Horn became very popular with the fans, because they knew he came to play. And Sam Horn never said no to anybody—anybody who wanted an autograph got one."

Horn began the 1988 season with the Red Sox. But he struggled, and soon was back in Pawtucket. The Red Sox eventually brought him back to the big leagues, but his playing time was select. Not accustomed to coming off the bench, he was disappointing in his sporadic plate appearances. In 24 games with the Red Sox, he hit just .148 with two home runs.

"I needed to play," said Horn. "But when Joe Morgan took over as manager, he was one of those guys who liked to play the veterans. If you were a veteran and you struggled, you got a chance to play. If you were not a veteran, you sat.

"That's just the way they did things in those days," he said. "You look at the Red Sox in recent years, and the way Grady Little and Terry Francona have used players, they were always moving different people in and out of the lineup. I might have flourished under those circumstances."

The Red Sox released Horn after the 1989 season. He was picked up by the Baltimore Orioles, for whom he played the next three seasons. In 1991, he hit a career-high 23 home runs in just 317 at-bats. He had a tour with the Cleveland Indians in 1993, this after hitting 38 home runs for the Tribe's Triple-A Charlotte club, and then ended his big-league career with the Texas Rangers in 1995.

But Horn was not forgotten by his New England fans, some of whom called themselves the Sons of Sam Horn. A website was launched paying homage to the Fenway Fridge, and, appropriately, it was called sonsofsamhorn.com.

The site's founder, Eric Christensen, is now Sam Horn's business partner. Reached by email, naturally, Christensen responded this way: "Ask a casual Red Sox fan if they remember Sam Horn and they'll look at you like you have three heads; ask a diehard Red Sox fan about Sam Horn and you'll have a half-hour conversation on your hands. Those are the kind of serious fans we want discussing all things Red Sox on the website, thus the name, 'Sons of Sam Horn.'"

Horn has big plans for the website, as well as for his career as a television personality. But there is a caveat to all this: Horn has not abandoned his hope to be back in uniform, and now dreams of being a big league hitting coach.

When he's not smiling for the cameras or keeping in touch with Sox fans via his website, Sam Horn, along with Debra, keeps busy with the couple's three children, Briona, Jamale and Kyla.

Where Have You Gone?

RAY CULP

R ay Culp was a solid pitcher during his days with the Red Sox, to say
nothing of the fact that his acquisition was a steal for general manager Dick O'Connell, who picked up the righthander from the Chicago
Cubs on November 30, 1967 for cash considerations and a minor-league
outfielder named Rudy Schlesinger, whose big-league career consisted of
just one at-bat.

That Culp is largely forgotten in Red Sox history has more to do with
bad timing than bad pitching. By joining the Red Sox just 49 days after
Game 7 of the 1967 World Series, he missed out on the team's 1967
pennant-winning "Impossible Dream" season, one of the most memorable in franchise history. And a long-simmering shoulder injury, which
Culp says he first suffered in high school, brought his career to an end
in 1973, just as the Sox were rebuilding for their historic showdown
against the Cincinnati Reds in the 1975 World Series.

"But I was with some very good Red Sox teams," said Culp, who,
other than when he was playing baseball, has lived his entire life in
Austin, Texas. "We went into every season believing we had a chance to
win. But every season I was there, somebody was better. The Tigers had
that great season in '68, and then the Orioles came along with all their
great players. In the end, we weren't good enough."

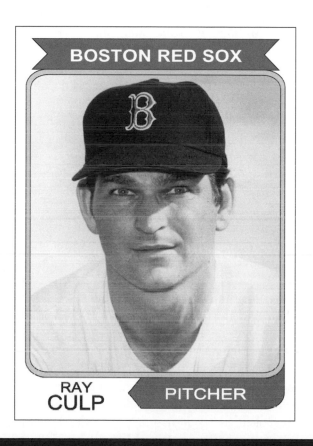

BOSTON RED SOX

RAY
CULP

PITCHER

RAY CULP
Years with Red Sox: 1968-1973

Best Season with Red Sox: 1969

• Games: 35 • Record: 16-6 • ERA: 2.91 • Innings Pitched: 216⅓ •
• Hits Allowed: 166 • Strikeouts: 190 • Walks: 82 • Complete Games: 11 •

After idling for a season with the Cubs, working out of the bullpen and as a spot starter, Culp found a home with the Red Sox. Looking for a change when he joined the team, he tossed out his old uniform number—37—and asked for a new one. Turns out that another Texas native, Cecil "Tex" Hughson, had worn the number in the 40s, so Culp snatched it up for himself. Years later, still another Texan, Roger Clemens, claimed the number—not because Hughson and Culp had worn it, but because it was his number at the University of Texas.

"I guess there's a lot of Texas in that number," said Culp. "But Roger's the one who made it famous."

Culp moved directly to the starting rotation for the 1968 Red Sox and came through with a 16-6 record. The next year he was 17-8, along with making a little personal history on August 9, 1969, when he cranked a pitch from California Angels rookie Pedro Borbon into Fenway Park's Green Monster for a home run—the only home run of Culp's career.

It so happened that the game was televised nationally as NBC's Saturday afternoon "Game of the Week," and Culp, after circling the bases, mentioned in the dugout that it was the *second* home run of his career. Somehow Culp's comment made its way up to the broadcast booth, and, after the game, the pitcher was interviewed by baseball legend Sandy Koufax, at the time a color analyst for NBC.

Koufax told Culp NBC had looked over the stats and had only come up with one home run, and then asked the pitcher about this phantom second four-bagger. To which Culp replied, "Oh, that was in a spring training game. But when you're as bad a hitter as I am, you count everything."

Culp, soft-spoken and good-natured, always preferred joking about his poor hitting than bragging about his excellent pitching. It was no surprise, then, that when Culp returned to Austin after his playing days and opened a real estate business, he named the company 123 Inc.—in honor of his career .123 lifetime batting average.

"More than a few people have asked if that's my earned-run average," Culp said. "I wish."

Born in Austin on August 6, 1941, Culp starred in baseball at Austin High School and then signed with the Philadelphia Phillies in 1959. He made his big-league debut in 1963 and pitched four seasons with the Phillies, and then was sent to the Cubs for pitcher Dick Ellsworth, who wound up joining Culp on the '68 Red Sox.

But Culp's shoulder had been bothering him since high school, and he believes he did yet more damage to it during his first season of minor-league baseball. The shoulder finally caught up with him near the end of the 1971 season—"I was pitching OK, but not throwing very well," he said—and he finally had to undergo surgery.

He never really made it back. He was 5-8 in 16 starts in 1972, where-upon the Red Sox released him and later re-signed him to a minor-league contract.

"They basically gave me a chance to go to Pawtucket and see what I could do," he said. He couldn't do much. He did get into 10 games with the Red Sox in '73, but was 2-6 with a 4.47 ERA.

He had won 64 games in his first four seasons with the Red Sox and had worked a scoreless inning (with two strikeouts) in the 1969 All-Star Game. Now he was 32 years old and done, and, as Culp put it, "I was way too young to be going home. I had planned on pitching a lot longer."

Fortunately, he had a home to go back to. He had married his high school sweetheart, and by the time he was finished pitching he and Sharon already had three daughters: Mitzi, Sherri and Tammi. After baseball, they proceeded to have three boys: Wes, Clint and Cody. Wes Culp pitched a couple of years in the Atlanta Braves system, and Cody Culp enrolled at Temple College in Temple, Texas, in the fall of 2004, planning to play baseball.

Culp's real estate business has done well—much better, in fact, than his hitting. He has dabbled in all kinds of real estate, from rentals to commercial properties, and the income allowed him to spend many years coaching his kids in baseball.

"I did it all, from tee-ball to Little League to Babe Ruth to Legion," he said. "I liked coaching. And I still love baseball."

Remember, though, that this is a man who pitched for a 1964 Phillies team that blew the National League pennant in the season's final weeks, and then played for the Red Sox post-1967 and pre-1975. So while the man has no regrets as to how his life *after* baseball turned out, he does add this: "I had a lot of success in the big leagues, but I never got a ring. That's my one regret."

Where Have You Gone?

LOU STRINGER

L ou Stringer had reached a point in his life where he figured folks didn't much care about his days as a professional baseball player.

He had put in parts of six seasons in the big leagues, including three with the Red Sox, in addition to carving out a distinguished career in the old Pacific Coast League, back when the PCL was considered by many to be "the third major league." But now he was a retired car salesman, living with his wife, Helen, in San Clemente, California, and, to be frank, his favorite anecdote had nothing to do with baseball, but, rather, the time he sold a Corvette to Elvis Presley.

But then, one day, while attending mass at Our Lady of Fatima Church in San Clemente, he met a fellow named Tony Ehlis.

"Tony was a baseball nut," said Stringer. "He was just obsessed with it, and when he found out I had played in the big leagues he was all over me. He'd come over to the house and look through all my old scrapbooks, and soon I was going over to his place, and soon we all became friends."

By "we all," Stringer was referring not just to the two men, but also to his wife, as well as Tony's wife, Wilma.

"Yeah, we all met through church and struck up a friendship," Stringer said. "We had a nice little gang."

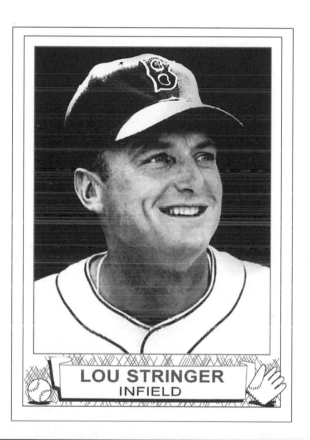

LOU STRINGER
Years with Red Sox: 1948-1950

Best Season with Red Sox: 1949

• Games: 35 • Batting Average: .268 • At Bats: 41 • Hits: 11 •
• Runs: 10 • Home Runs: 1 • RBIs: 6 • Slugging Percentage: .439 •

In 1989, Tony Ehlis passed away.

In 1993, Lou Stringer lost his beloved Helen.

But Lou Stringer and Wilma Ehlis continued to see each other at church, and the friendship grew. And in the unlikely event you haven't figured out where we're going with this, yes, Lou and Wilma eventually got married. They were hitched on November 19, 1994. As of December, 2004, they were living in El Toro, California, in a retirement community called Freedom Village. The betting here is that Lou and Wilma have a nice setup, seeing how Freedom Village is partly owned by Lou's son Tom.

"We're two very, very lucky people," said Stringer of his marriage to Wilma. "I guess you never know what's going to happen in your life."

Lou Stringer's life began on May 13, 1917. Born in Grand Rapids, Michigan, Stringer was just three years old when his parents, Robert and Josephine, packed up the family and moved to southern California.

"We moved because of my father's health," Stringer said. "My dad had a bad cough, and they thought the California climate would be better for him. We had a big family, seven boys and a girl, so it was a big move. We moved to 1338 East 48th Street in East Los Angeles, and I've pretty much been in California ever since."

Stringer signed with the Cubs in 1937 and made his big-league debut in 1941. He was the Cubs' everyday second baseman in '41, hitting .246 in 145 games. He was strictly a utility player in his three seasons with the Red Sox, a bench guy who had the best seat in the house while the big guys, including Ted Williams, did their thing.

"My memories of playing with the Red Sox mostly involve Ted Williams, because he was such a huge star," Stringer said. "One thing I'll never forget was being in the batting cage, and passing Ted as I came out. He didn't know me very well yet, and he said, 'Hey, you, who's the best hitter in baseball?' And I said, 'You are.' And he said, 'You're goddamn right I am,' as he walked away.

"Ted was a loner, though," Stringer said. "We'd all go out and eat dinner, except Ted. He kept mostly to himself, or he went fishing somewhere. And people weren't always fair to him. I went to a fight card in Boston with a couple of guys one night, and we ran into Ted there. Then they make this big announcement to introduce Ted, and they wanted him to come up to the ring and wave hello. Only he wasn't there. When he returned, the moment was over.

"The next day, one of the papers criticized him for not coming up to the ring. I asked him about it and he said, 'I was in the little boys' room. I wasn't even there when they introduced me.' So that wasn't right, what they said about him that night."

Stringer's stops in the Pacific Coast League included stints with the Los Angeles Angels, who with Lou on board won the league championship in 1947. He was with the Hollywood Stars in 1948, even managing the team for a while, when the Red Sox acquired his services. He also had stints with the San Francisco Seals and San Diego Padres.

It was while playing in the PCL that Stringer landed his first job as a car salesman. He was something of a local celebrity in Los Angeles-area sports circles, and his reputation as a ballplayer helped him move cars off the lot. He had a long career with Harry Mann Chevrolet in Los Angeles.

And now for the part you've been waiting for: Go ahead, Lou, tell us about your own personal Elvis sighting. (This one before Elvis died, of course.)

Photo courtesy of Lou and Wilma Stringer

"He called and ordered it over the phone," Stringer said. "He wanted me to drive it out to this place he was staying at in Hollywood and drop it off. So I drove the Corvette out there, and had a guy follow me in another car so he could drive me back to the dealership.

"When we got there, he gave me a check, and that was pretty much it. Turns out he bought the car so he could give it to some girl. He was nice, but I don't think he said 20 words while I was there."

In addition to his son Tom, Lou Stringer also has a daughter, Linda, who lives in Colorado. He has four grandchildren.

EDDIE PELLAGRINI

Nothing would have made Mary Pellagrini prouder than to see her boy, Eddie, attend college. And as she was a staunch Catholic living in the Dorchester section of Boston, she reasoned there was just one school for her son: Boston College.

"That was her dream," said Eddie. "She was a lovely, lovely lady, and she wanted me to be a success in life. And she always said she wanted me to study at Boston College."

Imagine, then, the poor woman's disappointment, when, following Eddie's graduation from Roxbury Memorial High School, the boy signed a contract to play baseball for the Boston Red Sox.

Baseball?

Mary had had all those dreams, all those hopes, and here now was her boy, her feisty little Eddie, playing . . . baseball!

And Eddie's father, Anthony Pellagrini, felt the same way. "He just never understood baseball," said Eddie. "He was a presser at Filene's Department Store in downtown Boston.

"He was a snappy little guy, a great dresser. Looked like a million bucks. But he didn't get baseball. Even when I finally made it to the big leagues and people would say, 'Hey, I went to the Red Sox game yesterday and saw your son play,' he wasn't impressed.

EDDIE PELLAGRINI
SHORTSTOP

EDDIE PELLAGRINI
Years with Red Sox: 1946-1947

Best Season with Red Sox: 1947

• Games: 74 • Batting Average: .203 • At Bats: 231 • Hits: 47 •
• Runs: 29 • Home Runs: 4 • RBIs: 19 • Stolen Bases: 2 •

"I don't think he ever figured out I got paid to play for the Red Sox," said Eddie. "He'd always say, 'He never works. He just plays baseball all the time.' After all these years, I still get a kick out of that."

It took a long time, but Eddie Pellagrini finally did make it to Boston College. After toughing out parts of eight seasons in the big leagues, mostly as a utility infielder, including two seasons with his hometown Red Sox, Pellagrini went into the real estate business. But in 1952, he received a fascinating offer: Boston College wanted to hire him as its baseball coach.

"I never wanted to leave baseball, but my wife, Helen, she didn't want me traveling," said Eddie. "So when the Boston College thing came along, it was perfect. I was being given a chance to coach baseball, yet still be able to live in Boston, and not have to travel so much."

Pellagrini figured he'd try the job for a couple of years. If it worked, fine. If not, well, what the heck: His mother would still be able to tell the neighbors her son had found respectable work at Boston College.

Couple of years? By the time Pellagrini retired, he had been Boston College's baseball coach for 31 years.

"And I honestly don't know which was the bigger thrill, playing for the Red Sox or coaching Boston College. I have fond memories of both. All those hundreds of kids I coached, they're like my own. A lot of them stay in touch. They write, they call. They're always looking out for me."

Despite battling a variety of health crises, Pellagrini was still keeping track of the Red Sox during the 2004 season, this after celebrating his 86th birthday. "Just a great, great show," he said. "I was born in 1918, when the Red Sox won the World Series, and I saw them win the World Series this year. That's pretty good, don't you think?"

Pellagrini began his professional career in 1938 with the Danville (Virginia) Leafs of the old Bi-State League. He made the league All-Star team at shortstop, and, as he proudly points out, "I hit 21 home runs that season. Can you imagine a little guy like me hitting 21 home runs? I still think that's unbelievable, that someone like me could ever hit one home run, to say nothing of 21 of 'em. I wasn't exactly Babe Ruth, you know."

It took eight years—including a four-year hitch in the Navy during World War II—before the man known locally as "Pellie" hit a much more memorable home run: Having finally made it on to the Red Sox' roster in 1946, Pellagrini became the seventh player in history to hit a home run in his first major-league at-bat. It was during an April 22 game against the Washington Senators at Fenway Park, off righty Sid Hudson, and it helped lead the Red Sox to a 5-4 victory.

"Now stop and think about that home run for a minute," said Pellagrini. "You're a kid from Boston, you've been kicking around for years in the minors, wondering if you're ever going to amount to anything, and now you're finally going to bat in the big leagues for the first time—for the Red Sox, and in Fenway Park. What a thrill."

Pellagrini thought he had made the Red Sox four years earlier. Uncle Sam, however, had different plans. With the war raging, Pellagrini returned to Boston from spring training and joined the Navy, and soon found himself at the Great Lakes Naval Station in Illinois. He was eventually shipped to Pearl Harbor. He played a lot of ball during the war, both at Great Lakes and at Pearl Harbor.

"I missed four years because of the war, but I have no regrets," said Pellagrini. "Obviously if I could have called the shots I would have played four or five years in the big leagues and then joined the navy, but, hey, you don't control those things.

"I often wonder if I might have had a better career had it not been for the war, but I have no complaints. I still played eight years in the big leagues, and that's something not a lot of people can say. And nobody can ever take that home run I hit off Sid Hudson away from me. You hold on to those things."

Pellagrini is a widower, his wife, Helen, having died in 1976. They had five children, including Celeste, who died in 1982, and Frannie, who died in 1989. They also had a set of twins, Michael and Maureen, and a daughter, Ann, who lives in Brighton, Massachusetts, and looks after her father.

"He made baseball his life," said Ann. "It was always important to him. It took me a long time, but now I know how significant it was that he played in the big leagues for all that time. So many of them didn't make it. My father is one of those who did make it."

Where Have You Gone?

JACK BAKER

In the early days of the 20th century, during baseball's deadball era, there lived a slugging third baseman from Maryland named Frank Baker. For four consecutive years he led the American League in home runs, including 12 during the 1913 season, powering the Philadelphia Athletics to a World Series championship.

Remember, this was before Babe Ruth was removed from the pitcher's mound and retooled as a longball threat. This was before Gehrig, before Hornsby. If you were talking home runs in those days, you were talking about Frank Baker. It was only natural, then, that the pundits started referring to the man as Frank "Home Run" Baker. Clever, no? As Casey Stengel used to say, you could look it up.

More than a half century later, a brawny young man from Alabama arrived at Auburn University to play baseball.

His name was Jack Baker. He could hit for power.

And it was only, natural, then, that the pundits called him Jack "Home Run" Baker.

Clever, no?

"I first heard that in college," Baker said. "Somebody wrote it in the campus paper, and it stayed around for a while. Then it went away for the longest time, until I was playing in the minors. And then people

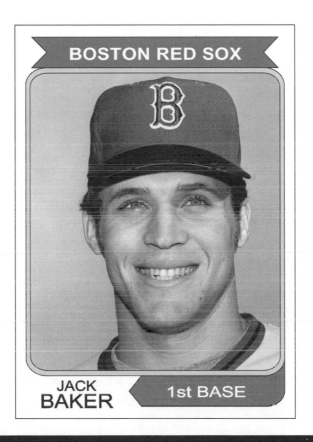

BOSTON RED SOX

JACK
BAKER   1st BASE

JACK BAKER
Years with Red Sox: 1976-1977

Best Season with Red Sox: 1976

• Games: 12 • Batting Average: .130 • At Bats: 23 • Hits: 3 •
• Runs: 1 • Home Runs: 1 • RBIs: 2 • Slugging Percentage: .261 •

from the various newspapers came up with it, so now I was Jack 'Home Run' Baker again."

Especially in 1976, when the 6-5, 225-pound first baseman, playing for the Pawtucket Red Sox, led the International League in home runs with 36. But more than earning him a nickname, his season also earned him a trip to the big leagues, where, on September 23, 1976, in the second inning of the Red Sox' 10-3 victory over the Milwaukee Brewers, Baker hit a home run over the Green Monster off lefthander Bill Travers.

"It was a fastball in," said Baker. "I remember it like it was yesterday."

Perhaps that's because it was the only major-league home run hit by Jack "Home Run" Baker, who a year later was traded to the Cleveland Indians. He never made it back to the big leagues with the Indians, and soon he drifted out of baseball. His career over before it ever really got going, Baker returned home to Alabama to help run his family's dairy business.

"You know, I tried a few years back to see if there was any film of that home run," Baker said. "I thought it might be nice for my kids to have. But it was a late-season game played between the Red Sox and Brewers, two teams that weren't going anywhere that year. The game wasn't on TV, so there's no footage of it anywhere. So all I have is my memory of it, and I guess that's OK. Each year, I add a few feet to it. By now, it's over the wall and bouncing around down on the Massachusetts Turnpike."

Baker's mission to retrieve an old piece of videotape is nothing compared to his mission back home in Alabama. A born-again Christian, Baker now works as area director for the Kansas City-based Fellowship of Christian Athletes.

"It's something I got involved with when I was in college," Baker said. "I had met Bill Glass, who played for the Cleveland Browns. He played his college football at Baylor, and his roommate was my cousin.

"When I was a young man, Bill made an impact on me," Baker said. "I knew then that Jesus was always going to be a part of my life. And later, when I was playing minor-league baseball, I visited these children at a school for the deaf and blind. And it showed me the impact that athletes can have on the lives of children.

"I remember reading that Charles Barkley said that athletes should not be role models for kids," Baker said. "I've always disagreed with that. Whether you like it or not, you're going to be role model. You don't have any say in the matter about being a role model. The only question is, are you going to be a good role model or a bad role model?"

Born in Birmingham on May 4, 1950, Baker was raised in a dairy family. Baker & Sons Dairy had been founded in 1895 by Baker's great-grandfather, and Jack, once his ballplaying days were over, went into the milk business. He eventually ran the company, with his brother, Bob, becoming vice president in charge of sales and marketing.

In 1996, the Bakers took a look at the books, and at the economy, and at the dairy business in general, and then made the painful decision to sell the company to Barber Dairies.

"It was the right thing to do," Baker said. "On the one hand, you're parting with a business that had been in your family since 1895. But the way the dairy business was going, we really had no choice. We might have been able to hang on for several more years, but then we ran the risk of walking away with nothing.

"By selling it at the time we did, we protected the jobs of 110 out of our 121 employees," he said. "And the employees who didn't move over to Barber either retired, took buyouts or accepted better-paying jobs elsewhere. Was it a sad time? You bet it was. But the right move. It was the right move."

Baker himself continued to work for Barber Dairies, eventually heading up its ice cream division. Barber then got bought out by Dean Foods, which eventually merged with the Dallas-based Suiza Foods, creating a national powerhouse.

But that's all in the past for Jack Baker. Today he's an ordained minister at McElwain Baptist Church in Birmingham, but he's often on the road, taking his work for the Fellowship of Christian Athletes to college campuses throughout the south.

He and his wife, Amy, have three grown children: Jeff, a project manager for a roofing company; Jenny, a CPA; and Sarah, who graduated from Auburn University in 2004.

Where Have You Gone?

TED LEPCIO

During the 1950s, when Red Sox great Ted Williams was waging war with the Boston media, the team had another Ted in the clubhouse who got along famously with the knights of the keyboard.

True, Ted Lepcio wasn't a star. He never hit .400, wasn't much of a power threat, and wasn't destined for the Hall of Fame, as was the better-known Ted who played for the Sox. As such, Ted Lepcio was neither a target of the writers nor a beneficiary of their kindness. He simply came and went through most of the '50s, an amiable middle infielder who never had a bad word to say about anyone, and who mixed well with everyone from teammates to managers, writers to fans.

Put another way, Thaddeus Stanley Lepcio was a natural-born salesman.

It should come as no surprise, then, that Lepcio went into sales after his playing career ended. But what may surprise you—unless you've had the pleasure of meeting this bouncy, pepper pot of a man—is that, even at the age of 74, Lepcio is still up with the sun each morning, still driving to work . . . and, yes, still selling.

As his wife, Martha, put it so well, "I don't think Ted is capable of slowing down. And it's good for him. Ted's one of those people who

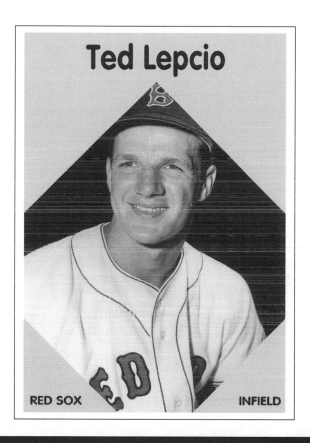

TED LEPCIO
Years with Red Sox: 1952-1959

Best Season with Red Sox: 1956

• Games: 83 • Batting Average: .261 • At Bats: 284 • Hits: 74 •
• Runs: 34 • Home Runs: 15 • RBIs: 51 • Slugging Percentage: .454 •

believes retirement is the great American killer, so he's going to keep working instead of staying home and watching television."

Lepcio is working these days for a Boston-based business known as Stonepath Logistics, a global transportation company. It's an industry with which Lepcio has a lot of experience: For more than 22 years he worked in sales for St. Johnsbury Trucking, helping, among other things, to develop a national accounts division for the company, which used to be located in Cambridge, Massachusetts, just across the Charles River from Fenway Park.

"I don't know if it was just the way I was born, or because of what I learned in college, or even because of my experience as a baseball player, but I always interfaced well with people," he said. "I guess it was a natural thing, but the baseball had to help. When you play in the big leagues, you're asked to deal with people every day. You have writers to talk to, and all the fans. I always believed it was much easier just to deal with people."

Born in Utica, New York, on July 28, 1930, Ted Lepcio was a standout baseball player at Seton Hall University. He was 20 years old when he signed with the Red Sox prior to the 1951 season, and he made his major-league debut just one year later, at age 21. And it wasn't just a cup of coffee: The kid (as opposed to The Kid, that being Williams) appeared in 84 games in '52, hitting a respectable .263 with five home runs in 274 at-bats, playing 57 games at second base, 25 games at third and a game at shortstop.

As such, Lepcio was that rare player who came up to the big leagues as a utility man and remained one throughout his career. He played 10 seasons in the big leagues, and though he had his share of success—he socked 15 home runs for the Red Sox in 1956—he had just one season (1954) when he registered more than 300 at-bats.

Early in the 1959 season, the Red Sox traded Lepcio to the Detroit Tigers. Over the next three years he bounced around from the Tigers to the White Sox to the Twins, but he had long since decided that, once his playing career ended, he would return to Boston and settle down.

"When I stopped playing, I went out and looked for a job, just like anyone else," he said. "I applied for a job with Honeywell Data Processing, and the fact that I had played for the Red Sox didn't even come up until the third interview.

"I ended up as a sales manager, and discovered that that's where I worked best," he said. "Again, it just comes down to working well with people. When I went to St. Johnsbury, I really found a home. I worked with some great people. The company's gone now, but I still get together with the old gang. We're like family."

Lepcio was a legend at St. Johnsbury. On the business side, he was a champion salesman. Away from work, he was virtually unbeatable in racquetball, as so many of his co-workers discovered.

"I still play a little," he said. "I have a bad knee, so I'm more into taking good, long walks. But I keep active."

Martha Lepcio was born and raised in Boston's West Roxbury section. She met Ted Lepcio through an acquaintance after Lepcio's baseball career ended, and they've been living in the Boston area ever since.

And after being a virtual stranger at Fenway Park for so many years, Lepcio, like a lot of ex-Red Sox players, has suddenly found himself welcomed back to the old ballpark.

"I can't say enough about the new owners," Lepcio said, referring to principal owner John Henry, club president Larry Lucchino and chairman Tom Werner. "It's not just that they finally found a way to win a World Series, though that's obviously a big part of it. But they've done something I believe to be very important: They've reached out to all the ex-players and made it known that we're welcome to be a part of things.

"It didn't used to be that way," he said. "Now, they invite us back and ask us to take part in the various things that they do there. It kind of makes you feel proud to be involved with the Red Sox."

And it's probably not bad for sales, either.

DENNIS ECKERSLEY

Dennis Eckersley retired from baseball at the end of the 1998 season, and it was only natural he'd go directly from the pitcher's mound to the television booth.

Surely the cameras would be keen on the Eck, an instantly-recognized baseball personality with good looks and a head of dark, wavy hair that famously twisted in the air each time he fired a fastball toward the plate. And it was a given that the microphones, too, would be attracted to Eckersley, who had always been outspoken, but, more than that, had his own unique way of saying even the simplest things.

While other pitchers tried to avoid giving up home runs, the Eck's mission was to "keep it in the yard." And, to him, a nothing-on-it fastball down the middle of the plate was, and is, "a cookie." A fastball with a little extra zip would be said to "have hair" on it.

True, other players have used these terms over the years. But as they say about the great stand-up comics, it's all in the delivery. When *Eckersley* talked about a fastball having hair on it, or "cheese," the lingo somehow had more meaning.

But Eckersley's transformation from pitcher to postgame television analyst on NESN, which televises Red Sox games on cable, was not

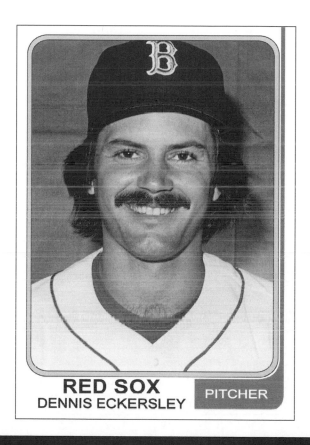

RED SOX
DENNIS ECKERSLEY   PITCHER

DENNIS ECKERSLEY
Years with Red Sox: 1978-1984, 1998

Best Season with Red Sox: 1978

• Games: 35 • Record: 20-8 • ERA: 2.99 • Innings Pitched: 268⅓ •
• Hits Allowed: 258 • Strikeouts: 162 • Walks: 71 • Complete Games: 16 •

without some struggle. He seemed uncomfortable at first, a little stiff. He was very un-Eck-like.

"It's not as easy as people think," he said. "It's one thing to sit around with a bunch of writers and just say whatever's on your mind, but, on television, with highlights playing and all that, it takes a while to sort everything out."

And, as anyone who knows Eckersley will tell you, "sorting things out" is something with which he has plenty of experience. More than being a guy who figured out how to make the transformation from player to television personality—which he did, so nicely settling into his NESN gig that he now says, "This is cake"—Eckersley has learned to sort things out in a variety of other areas in his life.

His made the transformation from All-Star starting pitcher to Hall of Fame closer. He rebounded from two failed marriages, one of which made headlines when it was revealed that his first wife was having an affair with Rick Manning, his teammate on the Cleveland Indians at the time. And, most important, he picked himself up off the ground, literally as well as figuratively, after years of alcohol abuse finally forced him to confront his demons and seek out a rehabilitation center. There have been setbacks along the way, but by 2004 Eckersley finally seemed to have things worked out: He was seriously involved with a new girlfriend, a lobbyist and spokesperson named Jennifer Szoke. The NESN career was going well. And on July 25, 2004, Eckersley, whose career seemed to be fizzling when the Red Sox traded him to the Cubs in 1984, was inducted into the Hall of Fame.

He's proud of his career. He's *really* proud of his sobriety. He's even involved in owning "sober living homes" in Cleveland, where he began his big-league career with the Indians in 1975.

"You've got these guys, and they're down and out, with no place to go, no place to sleep," Eckersley said. "I know something about that. I've been there. We run a good program. It's not state-funded. And that's good, because we don't have to deal with all the bureaucratic BS that goes with that."

Born in Oakland on October 3, 1954, Eckersley was selected in the third round of the 1972 amateur draft by the Indians. He was in the big leagues just three years later, going 13-7 in his rookie season. But his best season as a starter was with the Red Sox, after being traded to Boston before the 1978 season. He went 20-8 for the '78 Red Sox, and followed it up with a 17-10 record in 1979.

On May 25, 1984, he was traded to the Cubs.

"Tough trade," said Eckersley.

Tough city, too.

"For a guy who was drinking a lot, that wasn't the best place for me to be," he said. "Too many day games. You can get into a lot of trouble, and I did."

Just before the 1987 season, he was sent to the A's, along with a stumpy, hard-working utility infielder named Danny Rohn, for a couple of minor-leaguers. Eckersley wasn't happy about the A's decision to make him a relief pitcher, but the results proved to be historic: Eck's pitching style, as well as his temperament, was perfect for the bullpen. He emerged as the game's top closer for the next decade; though he will be remembered for the historic home run he gave up to Kirk Gibson in Game 1 of the 1988 World Series, it was also a season in which he registered 45 saves.

And in 1992, he was voted the American League's MVP *and* Cy Young Award winner after going 7-1 with a 1.91 ERA and 51 saves.

Though it was his years as a closer with the A's that landed him in the Hall of Fame, he has chosen to settle in Boston. "It's crazy here," he said, referring to the passion that New England baseball fans have for the Red Sox. "If you want to work in baseball, this is the place to be."

The Eck is a frequent visitor to the charity golf circuit, and he is now branching into corporate speaking, using his opportunities at the dais to lecture on his baseball career, of course, but also on his years-long quest for sobriety.

"There are so many opportunities, and, man, I have stories to tell," he said. "I've gone through a lot of stuff."

Eckersley has three children. His daughter Mandee was born in 1976, followed in 1980 by Jake and in 1996 by a second daughter, Allie.

And he still has the long hair.

JIM LONBORG

Jim Lonborg's baseball career ended on June 16, 1979. He had had a good run as a big-league pitcher, including a Cy Young Award-winning season with the 1967 Red Sox and, years later, two trips to the postseason with the Philadelphia Phillies, but now it was time to make some decisions about what to do with the rest of his life.

The first decision was reached in concert with his wife, Rosemary: Go on vacation. They returned to their home in Boston, found a babysitter to take care of the kids, and then hopped in the car and headed up to Vermont for a quiet getaway weekend.

Along the way, Rosemary volunteered her own thoughts about what her husband should pursue in the way of a post-baseball career.

"I think you should become a dentist," she said.

"A dentist?" asked Lonborg.

"Well, you've always wanted to work in the health field," she said. "And you always look great in uniform."

The idea made sense. Lonborg had been in pre-med during his Stanford days, and during off seasons as a member of the Red Sox he had found work at area hospitals, including one operated by Buddy LeRoux, a longtime Red Sox trainer who would eventually become a part-owner of the team.

JIM LONBORG
Years with Red Sox: 1965-1971

Best Season with Red Sox: 1967 (Cy Young Award Winner)

• Games: 39 • Record: 22-9 • ERA: 3.16 • Innings Pitched: 273⅓ •
• Hits Allowed: 228 • Strikeouts: 246 • Walks: 83 • Complete Games: 15 •

When Jim and Rosie returned to Boston, Lonborg got on the phone with Bill Lenkaitis, once a bruising center with the New England Patriots who had become a dentist after his own athletic career ended. His next step was to enroll for a semester at the University of Massachusetts at Boston in order to, as he put it, "get back in the groove again academically."

On one of his first days at UMass/Boston, in chemistry class, the professor passed a sheet of paper around the room, asking the students to jot down their names. When the paper reached Lonborg, he dutifully added his name and passed it to the next student.

A few minutes later, he heard a student say, "Oh, look, some asshole wrote down Jim Lonborg."

Lonborg survived his warm-up semester at UMass/Boston and enrolled in a three-year program at Boston's acclaimed Tufts University Dental School. Soon he was back in uniform again—albeit in a dentist's crisp white office coat—and setting up shop in the Boston area.

"I don't keep much in the way of baseball memorabilia in the office," Lonborg said. "I have the plaque in there from when I was inducted into the Red Sox Hall of Fame a few years ago, but that's about it.

"I want people to feel confident that I'm here to do dentistry, not anything else," he said.

Yet there's a facet to Jim Lonborg's life that gives him more joy than his dental practice, and even more joy than his distinguished 15-year baseball career, during which he won 157 games.

It's his family.

Concluding early on that they were unable to have children, Jim and Rosemary Lonborg looked to adoption as a passage to parenthood. In 1974, they adopted a baby girl, Phoebe. Two years later, they adopted two Korean babies, Nicholas and Claire.

And surprise, surprise: Exactly nine months to the day Nicholas and Claire were placed with the Lonborgs, Rosemary gave birth to a baby girl, Nora.

One year and three months later, she gave birth to a baby boy, John. And during her husband's last year at Tufts Dental School, she gave birth to another baby boy, Jordan.

The large, diverse Lonborg clan settled south of Boston in the town of Scituate, which, Dr. Lonborg says, "is one of the most beautiful, caring communities on earth. We're all very lucky and very happy the way things turned out."

Born on April 16, 1942 in Santa Maria, California, Lonborg took his skills—baseball as well as academic—to Stanford University before signing with the Red Sox in 1963. He was thrust into Boston's starting rotation just two years later, going 9-17, but in 1967 he had one of the greatest and most memorable seasons in Red Sox history, going 22-9 for the "Impossible Dream" American League pennant winners.

His 22nd victory came on the final day of the season, when he bested the Twins' Dean Chance to secure at least a tie for the pennant. The team then huddled around a radio in the Boston clubhouse, and celebrated wildly when a victory by the California Angels over the Detroit Tigers clinched the pennant for the 100-to-1 longshot Red Sox.

In addition to his pitching that day, Lonborg also delivered perhaps the most famous bunt in Red Sox history. Leading off the bottom of the sixth inning, the Red Sox trailing 2-0, Lonborg dropped a beauteous bunt down the third-base line in front of Twins third baseman Caesar Tovar and legged out a single. It was the beginning of a five-run rally for the Red Sox, and the beginning of the end for the Twins.

There was speculation in the old ballpark that a pinch hitter might come to the plate for Lonborg, but in *No More Mr. Nice Guy: My Life in Baseball*, by Dick Williams and Bill Plaschke, the former manager of the Red Sox writes of Lonborg: " . . . he had become one of my toughest and smartest players, and if anyone could figure out how to pull our ass out of the sling . . . well, he could and he did."

With a little less salt in his vernacular, Lonborg said, "I had worked on my bunting all season with (Red Sox coach) Bobby Doerr, so I wasn't clueless up there. And I saw that Tovar was playing a little deep, so I took a shot."

A much-publicized ski injury during the winter derailed Lonborg's career. He tore ligaments in his knee and struggled to a 6-10 record in 1968. He lasted three more seasons with the Red Sox before being traded to the Milwaukee Brewers, who kept the tall righthander for one season before sending him on to the Phillies.

Lonborg regained a measure of his old self with the Phillies, going 17-13 in 1974 and 18-10 in '76.

He still gets recognized in Boston as Jim Lonborg, baseball player.

"Sometimes, kids who weren't even born when I pitched for the Red Sox will say something to me," he said. "That's what being part of Red Sox history is all about. It gets passed on from parents to their kids."

Where Have You Gone?

DON GILE

The *Baseball Encyclopedia* is filled with the names of players who were dragged, kicking and screaming, from the game they loved so much.

They wanted to keep playing, these starry-eyed players did, but the ravages of time had other plans. Time leads to injuries, to failing eyesight, to increasingly uncooperative reflexes. And that's when you get called into the manager's office and are told it's over, time to go home, to get a real life.

Sure, a handful of players go out on their own terms. But those are the stars, the big names. Carl Yastrzemski. Cal Ripken Jr. Al Kaline. These guys go on a grand tour before they retire, and the big day invariably turns into an upper-case event, as in Carl Yastrzemski Day! Cal Ripken Jr. Day! Al Kaline Day!

But every once in a while, a player comes along who is far, far from being a star, but who still gets to determine when and how he will leave the game. That said, allow us to introduce the very unknown Don Gile, a onetime first baseman/catcher for the Red Sox who in the spring of 1963 had the temerity to tell the club that this would be his last season, thank you very much, that he'd be going home to California come October, not to return.

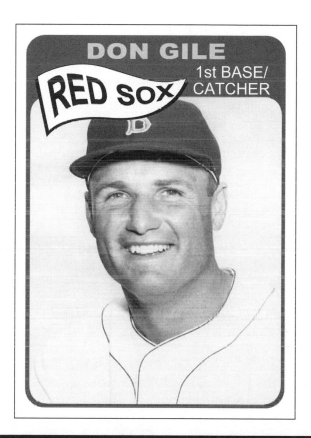

DON GILE
Years with Red Sox: 1959-1962

Best Season with Red Sox: 1961

• Games: 8 • Batting Average: .278 • At Bats: 18 • Hits: 5 •
• Runs: 2 • Home Runs: 1 • RBIs: 1 • Slugging Percentage: .444 •

"Well, I was 28 years old," Gile said. "And I was raised to believe that, no matter what you were doing, in baseball or in business, if you hadn't made it by the age of 30 then maybe it was time to think about doing something else. And looking back on my career at that time, I decided I had to think about the rest of my life."

For this, Gile had his father to thank. Victor Gile was a self-made man, a high school dropout who landed a low-level job with Bank of America and then had the smarts to turn his job into a career. He wound up staying with the bank for more than 50 years, ascending to vice-president status.

"It was," said Don Gile, "the only job he had ever had. And he knew at a young age he was going places, and he knew how to get there. That wasn't the case with me as a baseball player. I was married by then. I had kids. I wasn't making much money. I wasn't playing. I had to make plans."

Signed by the Red Sox in 1955 after playing baseball at the University of Arizona, Gile made it to the big leagues in 1959, appearing in three games. He also played in the big leagues in 1960, '61 and '62, but his playing time was spare; the most he ever played in a season was 29 games in 1960.

Having told the Red Sox he was going to retire after the 1963 season, he was, as he had expected, sent to the team's Triple-A farm club in Seattle. But then something strange happened: A little more than a month into the season, the Red Sox traded Gile to the San Francisco Giants, who sent him to their Triple-A farm club in Tacoma.

"It was amazing," Gile said. "One day I'm playing in Seattle, the next day I'm just a few miles south, playing in Tacoma."

But one aspect of the trade has always puzzled Gile: When the Red Sox made the trade, did they tell the Giants they had won the services of a player who was going to retire at the end of the season?

"That's a good one," said Gile. "I've often wondered that myself. But I believe they did tell the Giants what my plans were. Remember, it was just a minor-league trade, and I don't think it's like I was going to figure in the Giants' plans. If you look at what they had at the time, they already had a couple of guys named Willie McCovey and Orlando Cepeda to play first base. I believe they both wound up in the Hall of Fame.

"Everybody knew what my plans were," he said. "I had told the Red Sox in spring training, and I had also told my manager in Seattle, Mel Parnell. This wasn't a surprise."

Having made his decision to leave baseball, Gile's next task was to figure out what to do with his life. An old friend helped get him a sales job with Upjohn Pharmaceuticals, which led to a long, successful career. But while his father had settled in for a long stay at Bank of America, Gile, finding his niche in the drug industry, kept getting bigger and better opportunities.

He left Upjohn after four years to take a job with Squibb Pharmaceuticals, where he remained for six years. He then went to work for a German firm, Boehringer Ingelheim Corp., eventually moving into management, remaining four and a half years.

Next stop: Oral-B Laboratories, for whom he emerged as national sales manager in charge of both its dental and dermatology divisions. He stayed six years, and then took a job with Olsten Home Health Care, where he remained until 1996, when he retired.

Photo courtesy of Don Gile

"It was a good business to be in," he said. "You get to come in out of the cold, and you're in these nice, clean doctors' offices. Obviously, it was different from baseball. But do I miss baseball? I don't miss it the way you think. I have a hard time watching the games, because, having played, it's a different pace to me to be watching.

"But I miss the guys," he said. "I miss my teammates. I talk to some of them once in a while—Johnny Pesky, who managed me in Boston, and Dick Radatz, Jim Pagliaroni. But I miss that feeling of being on one team with a bunch of teammates who were your pals."

Gile was born on April 19, 1935 in Modesto, California, and raised in San Mateo. Today, he and his wife, Doris, live just south of San Francisco in Redwood City. They have four grown children.

Where Have You Gone?

LEE TINSLEY

When I spoke with Lee Tinsley in late November of 2004, just a couple of days after Thanksgiving, the former Red Sox outfielder was in a reflective—and thankful—mood.

He had just flown to Louisville from his home in Scottsdale, Arizona, to be with his father, Lee Tinsley Sr., who was being hospitalized after suffering an aneurism. Speaking from a telephone at the hospital, Tinsley said his father faced a long rehabilitation process, but added, "He's a strong man. He always has been. That's why I think he's going to be OK."

Any story about Lee Tinsley Jr., should begin with Lee Tinsley Sr., since, after all, it was the father who placed a love of baseball in his boy's heart. Never much of an athlete himself, just a regular guy who worked hard to provide for his family, the elder Tinsley was working at the Phillip-Morris plant in Louisville when he read an item in the local paper about baseball tryouts.

The father asked the son if he might be interested in playing the game. He didn't push the boy, didn't even nudge him. Just laid it out there for him: Do you want to play baseball?

"And I did want to play baseball," said Tinsley. "And that's when my father started making sacrifices for me so I could be the best baseball

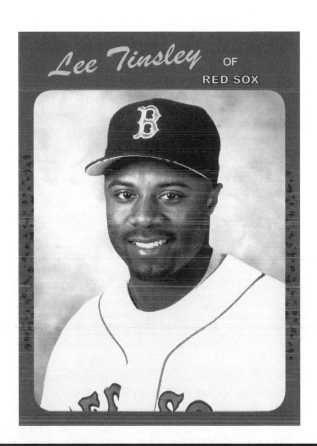

LEE TINSLEY
Years with Red Sox: 1994-1996

Best Season with Red Sox: 1995

• Games: 100 • Batting Average: .284 • At Bats: 341 • Hits: 97 •
• Runs: 61 • Home Runs: 7 • RBIs: 41 • Slugging Percentage: .402 •

player I could be. He was the first one to take me out and teach me how to throw a baseball. He was the first one to teach me how to swing a bat. He'd work from eight to three, and then we'd go play baseball, or he'd watch me play baseball."

Perhaps that's why Tinsley, who had two stints with the Red Sox in the '90s before ending his big-league career with the Seattle Mariners in 1997, is himself a teacher of baseball. Now working as a minor-league coach with the Arizona Diamondbacks, Tinsley's areas of expertise are outfield play, base running and bunting. He works throughout the D'backs' farm system, hoping to teach the same skills, as well as instilling the same values, that he learned growing up.

"I was lucky, because I had great coaches," Tinsley said. "It began with my father, but it continued when I was playing professionally. When I was drafted by the Oakland A's, I had Davey Nelson as a coach in the minors, and he was the kind of guy you wanted to listen to. I always felt that if I ever became a coach, I wanted to be like him.

"Later on, when I was with the Red Sox, I had Jim Rice and Mike Easler as coaches. Again, you listen to those guys."

Tinsley's own athletic career easily could have led to a career in football. Born on March 4, 1969, in Shelbyville, Kentucky, he was a multi-sport star at Shelbyville County High School, excelling in baseball, but also in football, basketball and track. He was offered a football scholarship by Purdue, but in the spring of his senior year, in his final high school baseball season, he hit .569 with 16 home runs and 65 RBIs. The Oakland A's selected him in the first round of the June amateur draft.

Four years later, the A's traded Tinsley to the Seattle Mariners, and it was with the M's that Tinsley made his major-league debut on April 6, 1993. But things didn't really kick in for Tinsley until 1994, when he was traded to the Red Sox. He was a reserve player for the Sox in '94, but in 1995 he became an everyday player for much of the season, appearing in 100 games and hitting a career-high .284, as well as having career highs in home runs (seven) and RBIs (41).

It was also the only season in which Tinsley appeared in the playoffs, as the Red Sox won the American League East championship before being eliminated by the Cleveland Indians in the Division Series. (One of the Indians' coaches in '95 was Davey Nelson, Tinsley's old minor-league mentor.)

"That season, that year, that was the best time of my life," he said. "Not only was I getting a chance to play, but I was playing a role on a winning team in a city that loves baseball. It was very special to me, and I wish it could have lasted forever."

It did not, of course. Tinsley was traded to the Phillies, and, though he was traded *back* to the Red Sox in June of 1996, he didn't get much playing time. It didn't help matters that he was playing with torn ligaments in his hand, which, as he looks back on those years, was probably a mistake.

He landed back with the Mariners in 1997. He appeared in just 49 games, hitting .197, and was released at the end of the season. He played a couple of seasons in Mexico, and in 2000 he hooked on with the Scottsdale Valley Vipers, an independent minor-league team managed by former A's pitcher Bob Welch.

And then Lee Tinsley retired. He was 31 years old.

"That was the tough part," he said. "You're out of baseball, and you look around and there are a lot of guys your age and older still playing. It's always a tough transition when you're still young at the end of your career."

But Tinsley and his wife, Susan, had more or less decided to settle in Arizona. He looked around for work as a coach, and the Diamondbacks offered him a job in their farm system. In 2001, he was hitting coach of the D'backs' Double-A El Paso team. In 2002, he took a job with the Anaheim Angels as a roving minor-league outfield coordinator.

"And both years," Tinsley pointed out, "the team I was working for won the World Series. I realize I was way down in the minors, but it was still fun to be part of a winning organization.

"I want to grow as a coach," he said. "I want to work at this and make something happen. I want it to be my career, but at the same time I want to give back. Do I want to be a major-league coach? Absolutely. And then we'll see what happens after that."

Tinsley returned to the Diamondbacks in 2003 and continues to coach in their farm system, as well as working as a hitting instructor in the Arizona Fall League. He and Susan have two children, Kobie, who turned six in 2004, and Ethan, who was born during the 2004 season.

Where Have You Gone?

JOHNNY PESKY

With their first selection in the June amateur draft in 2004, the Red Sox chose a five-foot-nine, 180-pound shortstop named Dustin Pedroia from Arizona State University. The 20-year-old native of Woodland, California, dutifully spent most of the summer playing errorless baseball in the lower rungs of the Red Sox' minor-league system, and then, in mid-September, came a surprise: The Sox brought the kid to Fenway Park to work out with the big club.

As Pedroia pulled his helmet down over his eyes and stepped into the batting cage, cracking line drive after line drive around the old yard, he did so under the astonished gaze of one Johnny Pesky, who was standing a few feet outside the first-base foul line.

"There it goes—another one!" hollered Pesky, leaning on his trusty, ever-present fungo bat.

"Another one!" the old man yelled. "And another one."

What a scene. What history. As Pesky spoke these words, he was just a few days shy of his 85th birthday. He had broken in as the Red Sox' shortstop in 1942, replacing the aging Joe Cronin, and now, 63 years later, he was standing on the field at Fenway Park, in full uniform, No. 6 on his back, shouting words of encouragement to a kid who may himself one day be the resident Fenway shortstop.

JOHNNY PESKY
SHORTSTOP

JOHNNY PESKY
Years with Red Sox: 1942-1952

Best Season with Red Sox: 1946 (All Star, 4th in MVP Voting)

• Games: 153 • Batting Average: .335 • At Bats: 621 • Hits: 208 •
• Runs: 115 • Home Runs: 2 • RBIs: 55 • Slugging Percentage: .427 •

"It was just incredible to meet him," said Pedroia. "I had heard about Johnny Pesky. I heard about Pesky's Pole at Fenway Park. But now I'm actually at Fenway Park, taking batting practice, and he walks up to me and introduces himself. How cool is that?"

Well, it's *real* cool, and the beauty of it all is that it is a regular occurrence at Fenway Park. For while Pesky's playing career ended in 1954 with the old Washington Senators, he happily settled into a new role as a baseball lifer. He coached and managed in the minor leagues. For two seasons, 1963 and '64, he managed the Red Sox. He was a big-league coach. He did a couple of years in the Red Sox' broadcast booth. Heck, in 1990, at 70 years old, he stepped in for half a season as manager of the Triple-A Pawtucket Red Sox. He continues to work for the Red Sox as a pregame coach, and all-around ambassador of goodwill.

"I guess they were never able to get rid of me," said Pesky. "They tried a few times, but I kept coming back. I guess I kind of go with the place."

What younger members of the Red Sox don't often know at first— and are sometimes astonished to discover—is that Pesky was one of the greatest players in Red Sox history. In fact, had it not been for World War II, during which Pesky missed three seasons to serve in the Navy, he may well have been enshrined in the Hall of Fame. As it was, he was a .307 lifetime hitter over 10 seasons, and in 1946 he hit .335 and teamed up with Ted Williams, Bobby Doerr and Dom DiMaggio to power the Red Sox to their first American League pennant since 1918.

"I know many, many players who, when they first got here, got to know Johnny a little bit and joked about it, and then looked up his numbers and realized what a tremendous player he was," said Red Sox general manager Theo Epstein. "It's always an eye-opening experience for them."

Born John Michael Paveskovich in Portland, Oregon, on September 27, 1919, Pesky was playing high school ball and working as a clubhouse kid for the Portland Beavers of the Pacific Coast League when he caught the eye of Red Sox scout Ernie Johnson. He made his big-league debut with the Sox in 1942, hitting .331 that season and amassing 205 hits.

But despite his fine career, Pesky's name will forever be attached to a play that occurred in Game 7 of the 1946 World Series. In the bottom of the eighth inning at Sportsman's Park, the St. Louis Cardinals' Harry Walker hit a liner to center field, whereupon Enos "Country" Slaughter, who was running on the pitch from first base, raced around the bases with what proved to be the winning run.

The myth goes like this: Pesky took the relay from center fielder Leon Culberson and "held" the ball, allowing Slaughter to score. The reality is much different. Films of the play do not show Pesky holding the ball; moreover, it's likely Slaughter would not have kept running had it been Dom DiMaggio, and not Culberson, in center field. But DiMaggio had pulled a muscle the previous inning and now it was Culberson, whose arm did not match DiMaggio's, in center field.

At best, Pesky, who had his back to the plate when he collected the ball, may have hesitated for a moment as he looked for Slaughter. It should be pointed out, too, that Culberson, who had the play in front of him, apparently hollered nothing to Pesky. But the myth grew over the years, and remains a part of baseball lore.

One of the most oft-told stories in the aftermath of the 1946 World Series places Pesky in the stands at the annual Oregon-Oregon State football game. It was said to be a rainy, windy, muddy day, with fumbles

Photo courtesy of Johnny Pesky

galore, inspiring one leather-lunged fan to stand up and yell, "Give the ball to Pesky—he'll hold onto it!"

So, did it happen?

"Yes, it did," Pesky said. "And, you know, to this day there's still someone that'll come up to me once in a while and say, 'Well, there's the guy who blew the '46 World Series.'"

Pesky can laugh at it all now. You don't live to be 85 years old by sweating the small stuff. It doesn't hurt that Pesky has had his wife Ruthie to keep him in line, along with their son, David, who, Pesky said, ". . . works at the State House. He's one of those guys you call when you have something to complain about."

What Pesky rarely talks about is that David is adopted.

"Ruthie and I had been trying to have a baby," he said, "and one day the priest who married us brought up the idea that we might consider adoption. Well, we did look into it, and then one day we went into Boston and saw that little baby and we just fell in love. He's all grown up now, but he calls his mother every day."

He continues to be an amazing man, Johnny Pesky. And the added bonus is that he's the only man in baseball to have a foul pole named after him. The legend goes that Pesky, never a power hitter, managed to wrap a couple of home runs around the right-field foul pole at Fenway, inspiring pitcher Mel Parnell to come up with the name "Pesky's Pole."

Pesky's Pole will forever be a part of Fenway.

So, too, will the man for whom it's named.

TOM SATRIANO

Tom Satriano has told the joke so many times over the years that he delivers it with the pacing, facial gestures and voice inflections of a seasoned comedian. He'll start by waxing poetic about his own baseball career, how he grew up in Pittsburgh, played college ball at the University of Southern California, and then made it to the big leagues.

He'll then talk about his life after baseball, followed by a discussion about his five children.

"You know, I played a couple of seasons with the Red Sox, and they were the happiest years of my career," he'll say. "I loved playing at Fenway Park. And I always dreamed that, one day, one of my kids would play at Fenway."

Pause.

And then, perfect every time, comes the punch line.

"I just didn't think it would be my daughter."

And everyone laughs. Every time. Because it's true.

Gina Satriano, daughter of the former big-league catcher, was herself a fine athlete growing up in southern California. She played Little League baseball in Brentwood, and, later, at Santa Monica High School. When she arrived at the University of California/Davis, she switched to softball.

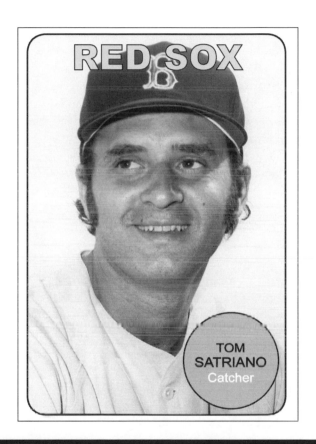

TOM SATRIANO
Years with Red Sox: 1969-1970

Best Season with the Red Sox: 1970

• Games: 59 • Batting Average: .236 • At Bats: 165 • Hits: 39 •
• Runs: 21 • Home Runs: 3 • RBIs: 13 • Slugging Percentage: .358 •

But then, after Gina had completed college and earned her law degree from Pepperdine and was working as a deputy district attorney for Los Angeles County, she heard about a new professional baseball team that was being organized. Unlike the long-ago All-American Girls Professional Baseball League, which operated in different forms from 1943 to 1954, with such exotic-sounding teams as the Rockford Peaches and Kenosha Comets, the idea this time was to form a barnstorming club that would take on all comers from coast to coast.

And so it was that the Colorado Silver Bullets were hatched, playing their first game in 1994. Gina Satriano, putting her law career on hold, played two seasons with the Bullets, pitching mostly in relief. In '94, she had the second lowest ERA on the team.

How did Dad feel about his daughter barnstorming across the United States as a professional baseball player?

"Oh, I was thrilled," he said. "She played in a lot of big-league ball-parks—Fenway, Shea Stadium. It was a big thrill to see my daughter play in some of the ballparks I played in."

After her baseball career ended, Gina Satriano resumed her work as a deputy district attorney. In 2001, she prosecuted the case of comedian Paula Poundstone, who was convicted of child endangerment.

In addition to his baseball-playing daughter, Satriano has five other children—Lisa, Nick, Anthony, Amber and Gianna. Nick Satriano played baseball at the University of California/Santa Barbara.

Thomas Victor Nicholas Satriano was born in Pittsburgh on August 28, 1940. Following his baseball career at USC, he signed with the Los Angeles Angels. When he made his major-league debut with the Angels on July 23, 1961, he was just 20 years old.

He played nine seasons with the Angels, both in Los Angeles, and, later, in Anaheim. His best season was 1968, when he appeared in 111 games and hit .253 with eight home runs with 35 RBIs.

On June 15, 1969, he was traded to the Red Sox for catcher Joe Azcue. Though he was mostly a backup during the parts of two seasons he played with the Red Sox, he emerged in 1970 as the pet catcher of pitcher Sonny Siebert, who went 15-8. Satriano, grateful for the occasional playing time, hit .236 in 59 games.

"The thing about me catching Sonny Siebert all the time, that actually happened by accident," said Satriano. "I was talking with him one day out in the outfield, and I told him he should be challenging hitters more. Well, I ended up catching him his next start, and he threw a two-hitter or something like that. From then on, our manager, Eddie Kasko, usually had me catching when Sonny pitched."

Like so many big-leaguers, Tom Satriano never made it to the post-season. The closest he came was in 1967, when the Angels wound up finishing seven and a half games out of first place in a wild pennant race that saw the "Impossible Dream" Red Sox emerge in first place. And though he played for some good teams with the Red Sox, those teams weren't good enough.

"The Orioles were the best team in the American League when I was playing for the Red Sox, so we weren't fighting for the pennant," he said. "But you know what? We were 20 games out of first place, and Fenway Park was still packed and everyone in town was talking about us all the time. It was a big difference from my years with the Angels. It wasn't like that in Anaheim.

"I made some good friends with the Red Sox. I played a lot of bridge with Carl Yastrzemski. I palled around with Rico Petrocelli, who had a terrific season in '69. My roommate was George Thomas, and he was a crazy guy. So there was never a dull moment."

But as much fun as Satriano had playing for the Red Sox, he was already planning to do other things with his life. After all, he knew he wouldn't get rich playing baseball: The most he ever made in a season was $34,000, and that was with the Red Sox in 1970, his last season.

"I was working as an accountant for Price Waterhouse during the off season, and I knew early on that there was a career there waiting for me," he said. "So I eventually became a CPA and started my own practice."

The business he started was UHY Advisors Inc., which he sold in 2000, after 25 years.

"But that doesn't mean I'm retired," Satriano said. "I still do a lot of consulting. I'm busier now than I've ever been."

Though he didn't plan to go work for the company he once owned, that's precisely what happened. He continues to do tax preparation, estate planning and other chores at the accountant's rock pile—very much un-retired as he closes in on his 65th birthday.

Where Have You Gone?

JIM GOSGER

J im Gosger was never much of a hitter, logging just a .226 average in
the parts of 10 years he played in the big leagues. But he was a good
listener, so when former Red Sox great Ted Williams offered him some
free advice one day, Gosger, a kid in his early 20s, eagerly listened.

"Ted was a coach with the Red Sox in spring training," Gosger said.
"What he said to me was that if I was having trouble with outside pitches I should try moving my back foot in a little. So I gave it a try, and I
had some success."

Now, let's fast forward about 40 years, to October of 2004. Gosger,
his baseball days long over, is living in the house in which he grew up in
Port Huron, Michigan. He's retired from his job with the utilities division of the city of Port Huron, but he's not retired from life: Divorced
and remarried, he and his wife, Kathleen, have a daughter, Kellie.

So there's Gosger, watching the Red Sox play the Yankees in the
American League Championship Series, and he notices that outfielder
Johnny Damon, coming off a superb regular season, is struggling in the
playoffs. And Gosger, sitting there in his easy chair, notices something.

"I thought he was having trouble with pitches on the outside of the
plate, and I started to remember what Ted Williams told me," said
Gosger. "I was sitting there, saying he should move his back foot a little,

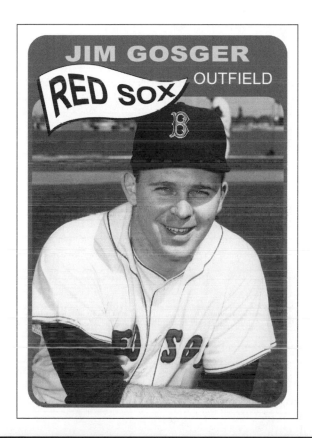

JIM GOSGER
Years with Red Sox: 1963-1966

Best Season with Red Sox: 1965

• Games: 81 • Batting Average: .256 • At Bats: 324 • Hits: 83 •
• Runs: 45 • Home Runs: 9 • RBIs: 35 • Slugging Percentage: .410 •

and my daughter said to me, 'Well, if you're so sure of that, you should get in touch with him and let him know.'"

"I don't know how to get in touch with Johnny Damon," said Gosger.

"You could send him an email," said Kellie.

Partly as an exercise to spend some quality time with his daughter, and partly out of genuine curiosity, Jim Gosger, a few weeks shy of his 62nd birthday, sat down with his 14-year-old daughter and crafted an email to Johnny Damon and sent it on its way to the Red Sox.

A couple of nights later, Gosger and his daughter sat down to watch Game 7 of the American League Championship Series, Red Sox vs. Yankees. And before we go any further with this, yes, absolutely, Gosger was rooting for the Red Sox. Even though he did a lot of bouncing around in his career—Kansas City Athletics, Oakland Athletics, Seattle Pilots, New York Mets, Montreal Expos—it was the Red Sox who first signed Gosger, and who first brought him to the big leagues, so, yes, he was rooting for the Sox to overtake the Yankees. Even Kathleen got into the act, going to work wearing a Red Sox uniform top her husband had worn 10 years ago at an oldtimers game.

"So the game begins," Gosger said, "and Damon gets a single in his first at-bat . . ."

It gets better. In the second inning, Damon rifled a grand slam to right field off Yankees reliever Javier Vazquez. In the fourth inning, also against Vazquez, Damon hit a two-run homer.

Three at-bats. Three hits. Two home runs. Six RBIs. And it all made Gosger wonder: Did Damon read the email that had been dispatched by the old baseball player?

"I don't think there's any question he moved his back foot," said Gosger. "I could tell by watching the games on television. But whether or not he got my email, I don't know. All I know is that I had some advice that had been given to me by Ted Williams, and, what the heck, I wanted to see to it that it got passed on."

Had things gone the way he had envisioned them, Gosger would be making a living handing out batting tips. Released by the Mets following the 1974 season, he was promised a coaching job by the club, he said, something about being a minor-league hitting instructor.

"They said they were going to call me," Gosger said. "That was in 1974. Here it is, 30 years later, and I'm still waiting for that call."

Instead, Gosger drifted into amateur officiating, becoming a well-known high school basketball and football referee in Michigan. He also does junior college games.

"But it's not like it used to be," Gosger said. "The players are a lot more brash than they were when I was coming along. We had one coach here, a few years back, and in the heat of the moment he grabbed a kid by the shirt. The family was going to press charges unless the guy quit coaching, which is what happened.

"When I was playing, if you mouthed off to a coach he'd grab you and throw you up against a locker," Gosger said. "And if you went home and told your father about it, he'd kick your butt. Sorry, but I think things were better that way."

Born on November 6, 1942, in Port Huron, Gosger signed with the Red Sox in 1962. When he made his big-league debut on May 4, 1963, he was just 20 years old. He was traded to the Kansas City A's in 1966 for outfielder Jose Tartabull and pitchers Rollie Sheldon and John Wyatt. While Tartabull and Wyatt went on to play key roles in the Red Sox' 1967 pennant run, Gosger became a baseball drifter for the remainder

Photo courtesy of Jim Gosger

of his career, culminating with the promise of a telephone call from the Mets that has yet to arrive.

But he received another, more important telephone call that changed his life. Divorced by then, and the father of four children, he was asked by a friend if he wanted to be fixed up on a blind date. The blind date led to a second date, and then a third, and today Jim and Kathleen have their hands full with Kellie, who just entered high school.

"I have one daughter who's 40, and another daughter who's 14," said Gosger. "And I figure if I'm young enough to have a 14-year-old daughter, I'm young enough to still coach baseball. And I'd love to work with those kids in the minors."

Perhaps Jim Gosger should call the Red Sox about a job.

Better yet, maybe he should just send them an email.

Where Have You Gone?

JERRY REMY

Howard Cosell was a bigger-than-life broadcaster who enjoyed cozy-ing up to bigger-than-life athletes. Think Muhammad Ali. Think Joe Namath.

Yet during the years in which the brash, flamboyant Cosell was behind the mike for ABC's *Monday Night Baseball* telecasts, one of his favorite players was a five-foot-nine, 165-pound second baseman from Swansea, Massachusetts.

Howard Cosell? With Jerry Remy? Shouldn't Cosell have been hang-ing around with Carl Yastrzemski? Jim Rice? Fred Lynn? Luis Tiant? Carlton Fisk?

Jerry Remy?

"Howard always liked me," said Remy. "He was always coming up to me and putting his big arm around me, saying hello. But I think part of the reason he liked me so much is that I didn't mind when he was reach-ing into my locker for a cigarette.

"He was always saying, 'Hey, Remy, give me a cigarette.' Either that, or he'd just go get one himself."

Either because of Remy's relationship with Cosell, or more than like-ly in spite of it, the smallish second baseman went on to become a giant of a broadcaster himself. No disrespect to the late, great Cosell, who was

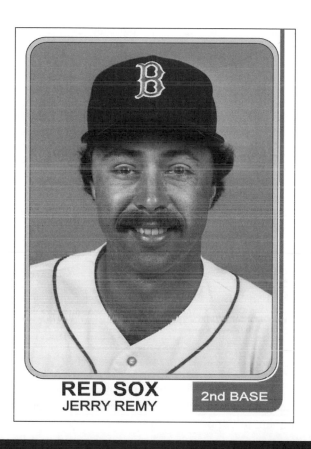

RED SOX
JERRY REMY

2nd BASE

JERRY REMY
Years with Red Sox: 1978-1984

Best Season with Red Sox: 1982

• Games: 155 • Batting Average: .280 • At Bats: 636 • Hits: 178 •
• Runs: 73 • Home Runs: 0 • RBIs: 47 • Slugging Percentage: .337 •

never afraid to offend people, but the big difference between the two men is this: People actually *like* Remy.

And that's being calm with the praise. Remy, who has been a color analyst in the Red Sox' broadcast booth since 1988, has developed a cult-like following throughout that ever-expanding place called Red Sox Nation. More than merely being a popular television personality, Remy has a website, TheRemyReport.com, that reaches thousands of fans each day. He has written a local bestseller, *Watching Baseball,* aimed at Red Sox fans, and he branched out yet again in 2004 when the man known as the RemDawg opened a concessions stand outside Fenway Park. Naturally, RemDawgs are the big-ticket item on the menu.

"I never expected this, not in a million years," said Remy. "It's certainly not something I ever planned. It just sort of happened. And it keeps happening."

Consider, for instance, one of the most popular items for sale at Remy's site: Copies of the old ballplayer's scorecard from any game he has worked. For $14.95, fans can get an autographed copy of a Remy scorecard, with a portion of the proceeds going to the Jimmy Fund, the fundraising arm of the nationally acclaimed Dana-Farber Cancer Institute.

Imagine: You and your date have attended a Red Sox game, and now you want something special to commemorate the occasion. To thousands of Sox fans, that "something special" has been a copy of a Remy scorecard. Only in America, no?

"The bigger the game, the more scorecards people want to buy," Remy said. "Derek Lowe's no-hitter (in 2002) was a big seller. And I signed so many cards after the Red Sox won the World Series I thought my arm was going to fall off."

Yet it's possible none of this would have happened had Remy landed the minor-league managing job he had been seeking. Having battled a series of knee injuries for years, Remy finally retired during spring training in 1986 and was offered a job as a coach with the team's Double-A club in New Britain, Connecticut.

"At that point in my life, with my playing career over, my goal was to be a big-league manager," he said. "That seemed the logical thing for me to do."

After one season at New Britain, it was with major-league ambitions that Remy applied for a minor-league managing job, hoping to be named skipper of the Sox' Triple-A club in Pawtucket, Rhode Island.

The job would have been perfect for Remy on two levels: One, he'd be a step away from the big leagues, and, two, he'd be able to commute to Pawtucket from his home outside Boston.

After interviewing Remy and other candidates, the Red Sox hired Singin' Ed Nottle, a longtime minor-league manager and occasional lounge crooner who had cut his own album, titled "To Baseball With Love."

"When I didn't get the job, I went home and basically did nothing for a year," said Remy. "But it's weird how things happened. A year later, NESN hired me to work in the television booth, even though I didn't have any experience. And that's what I've been doing ever since.

"Let's say I had been hired to manage Pawtucket," Remy said. "Well, maybe I have some success, and maybe I end up managing in the big leagues. But like just about everybody, I'd have managed for a few years and then I would have been fired.

"I'd have to say this worked out pretty good for me," he said.

Born in Fall River, Massachusetts on November 8, 1952 and raised in nearby Somerset, Remy naturally grew up a Red Sox fan. And long before he actually played for the Red Sox, he played a cameo role in the team's history: On October 1, 1967, when the Sox defeated the Minnesota Twins to clinch at least at least a tie for the American League pennant, a 14-year-old Jerry Remy was among the thousands of fans who stormed onto the Fenway Park lawn.

Selected by the California Angels in the eighth round of the 1971 amateur draft, Remy made his major-league debut in 1975, when he was just 22. He was traded to the Red Sox after the 1977 season for pitcher Don Aase.

Remy and his wife, Phoebe, have three children: Jared, born in 1978; Jordan, born in 1980; and Jenna, born in 1984.

And while most Red Sox fans were stunned when, in 1978, the New York Yankees stormed into Fenway Park and annihilated the Sox in a four-game series that came to be known as The Boston Massacre, Remy's first son, Jared, was born after the opening game of the historic mismatch.

"I was out with a wrist injury, but available for pinch-running duty," Remy said. "I was there for the game, but didn't play. But I made it to the hospital to see my son. So the week wasn't all bad."

MATT BATTS

Matt Batts was a tough, fire hydrant of a big-league ballplayer, a 5-11, 200-pound catcher who left Baylor University because he wanted to play with the Boston Red Sox. And he achieved his dream, logging parts of five seasons with the Red Sox from 1947 to 1951 before bouncing around for a few years with the St. Louis Browns, Detroit Tigers, Chicago White Sox and Cincinnati Reds.

As catchers go, he wasn't bad, logging a respectable .269 lifetime batting average. He had a little pop in his bat—he had six home runs and 26 doubles with the Tigers in 1953—and he was a capable defensive catcher.

Yet in order to discuss the greatest athletic achievement in the career of Matthew Daniel Batts, we don't have to go back as far as the '40s and '50s. And we don't even need a copy of the *Baseball Encyclopedia*, or a visit to baseball-reference.com.

But a workingman's knowledge of golf wouldn't hurt.

Golf?

"I'd play it seven days a week if I could," said Batts, who turned 83 on October 16, 2004 and, naturally, celebrated the occasion with a round of golf. It should come as no surprise, then, that he and his wife,

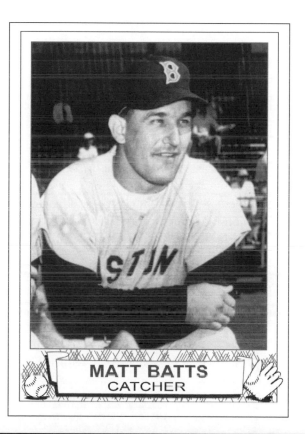

MATT BATTS
CATCHER

MATT BATTS
Years with Red Sox: 1947-1951

Best Season with Red Sox: 1948

• Games: 46 • Batting Average: .314 • At Bats: 118 • Hits: 37 •
• Runs: 13 • Home Runs: 1 • RBIs: 24 • Slugging Percentage: .441 •

Arleene, live in a gated community at The Country Club in Baton Rouge, Louisiana, where the links are right out the back door.

Now, about that greatest athletic achievement, or, as Batts pointed out, "Actually, it was two great achievements, and I don't know which one makes me the most proud."

You decide.

Athletic achievement No. 1: Playing at the nearby Beaver Creek Golf Course in the summer of 2004, Batts reached for his trusty 6-iron and registered his first ever hole in one.

"It was the third hole, about 145 yards," Batts said. "I hit it good, but I thought it kind of doved to the right and then I couldn't see the ball. I thought maybe it went into the rough. One of my friends said, 'I think that ball's in the hole, and that's where you should look for it.' I laughed, figuring I wasn't about to get a hole in one at my age. Sure enough, I got down there and looked in the hole, and I said, 'Gahl'dang, there it is.'"

Athletic achievement No. 2: In October of 2004, shortly before his 84th birthday, back on his home turf at The Country Club, Batts shot an 83. Yep: The man shot his age, something not often done.

"It was just of those things," he said. "Sometimes you have a good day. Everything seemed to be going right. I came home and told Arleene, and she just said, 'Yeah, right.' Even my wife didn't believe me."

Batts owes his great golf game to his leisure time, and he owes his leisure time to his decision to open a printing business after his baseball career ended. His last year in the big leagues was early in the 1956 season with the Reds, after which he and Arleene returned home to Baton Rouge.

He tried his hand in politics for a while, running for local constable after working as an investigator for the district attorney's office, but he said he "lost the race by 115 votes, and that was enough of politics for me. I decided I wanted to do something else with my life where I could have more control over things."

He and his wife opened a business, Batts Printing Company, which proved to be a success.

"And that printing business is why I'm able to play so much golf," he said with a big laugh. "It certainly wasn't from the money I made playing baseball. When we sold the business, that's when my golf game picked up. I had started golfing when I was with the Red Sox. I picked it up from some of the guys in the clubhouse. I never thought I'd grow to be so passionate about it."

Born in San Antonio, Texas, in 1921, Batts played both baseball and football at Baylor University until he left school to sign with the Red Sox. He also served three years in World War II, flying B-25s at a training base in Texas, and then made his major-league debut late in the 1947 season with the Red Sox.

"Boston was a fine place to play," said Batts. "The best thing is, they treated rookies with respect. You'd hear all kinds of stories about rookies on other teams getting pushed around by the veterans. But that wasn't the case with the Red Sox. Ted Williams and Johnny Pesky and those guys treated me well."

Matt and Arleene spent one winter in Boston.

"And I do believe it was the coldest winter in the history of Boston," said Arleene. "That was enough for us. Boston's a lovely city, but it was not where we needed to be in the wintertime."

They returned to Baton Rouge and settled down. They have two daughters and four grandchildren, one of whom has since relocated to Boston, where she works as a dental assistant.

Photo courtesy of Matt Batts

"You'd think nobody would remember my grandfather," said Jary Claflin, whose late uncle, Larry Claflin, was a well-known Boston sports columnist in the '60s and '70s. "But sometimes I'll mention his name to some of our older patients, and they'll light up. We had one patient who said my grandfather once threw a ball to him.

"I enjoy being in Boston, but I also enjoy the connection my grandfather has with this city, and the fact that there are still people here who knew him. And I love telling people his baseball stories."

All well and good. But if she really wants to make her grandfather a happy man, she should tell people about his golf game.

Where Have You Gone?

LUIS TIANT

L ate in his career, Luis Tiant chose to leave the Red Sox. But he never
really left Boston. Having resurrected his career as a member of the
Red Sox in the early '70s, the amiable, cigar-smoking Cuban settled
down in the Boston area, and he has more or less continued to live within an easy drive of Fenway Park since the day he threw his last pitch in
the big leagues.

If you're a Red Sox fan, you can't get away from the guy. Take a trip
to Fenway Park and visit Yawkey Way, which gets transformed into a
hardball street fair on game days, and you can buy a Cuban sandwich
and other goodies at "El Tiante's."

Or you can step inside tobacco stores in the Boston area and purchase a genuine Luis Tiant cigar.

Tiant has worked as a color analyst for the team's Spanish radio network. He has made appearances for NESN, the team-owned cable out-
let for Red Sox games. He is a frequent guest at banquets, fantasy camps
and various first-pitch ceremonies. He has been a minor-league pitching
coach, and each spring works with some of the veteran pitchers in big-
league camp. Tiant also made a curious career decision when he coached
the baseball team at the Savannah College of Art and Design from 1999
to 2002, but he continued to make Boston his home.

BOSTON RED SOX

LUIS TIANT | PITCHER

LUIS TIANT
Years with Red Sox 1971-1978

Best Season with Red Sox: 1974 (All Star, 4th in Cy Young voting)

• Games: 38 • Record: 22-13 • ERA: 2.92 • Innings Pitched: 311⅓ •
• Hits Allowed: 281 • Strikeouts: 176 • Walks: 82 • Complete Games: 25 •

And why not? During his days with the Red Sox, Tiant was as much the public face of the organization as any of the team's powerful offensive stars. Fans grew accustomed to his twisting motion as he delivered each pitch to the plate—it was said that he could look directly into the eyes of folks in the center-field bleachers while in his windup—and the famous "Looooie! Looooie! Looooie!" chant that rose from the Fenway stands became a New England anthem of the '70s.

Yet when he arrived in Boston in 1971, he was an aging pitcher who had been cast aside by two other organizations within a span of six weeks. And from a statistical standpoint, he did little with the '71 Red Sox to suggest he was going to regain his old form. This is a guy who as recently as 1968 had given the Cleveland Indians a 21-9 record and an American League-leading 1.60 ERA; now he was a sometimes-starter and mop-up guy for the Red Sox, and the best he could do was a 1-7 record and 4.85 ERA.

Part of the problem was that Tiant was attempting a comeback from a broken clavicle. But the Minnesota Twins had given up on him in spring training, forcing Tiant to sign a deal with the Atlanta Braves' Triple-A Richmond club. The Braves released him, and now it was the Red Sox who took a shot.

"I needed innings," Tiant said. "I needed to pitch and get my rhythm back. I hadn't done much relief pitching before, but I did a lot of that for the Red Sox that first year."

It turned out to be one of the best acquisitions in Red Sox history. Tiant gave the Red Sox a 15-6 record in 1972, and his 1.91 ERA was again the best in the American League. Tiant went on to win 20 or more games in three of the next four seasons, remaining with the Red Sox through the infamous 1978 season. His career record with the Red Sox was 122-81, a .601 winning percentage. Not bad for a guy rescued from the Triple-A trash heap.

Tiant's lasting legacy with the Red Sox will be his status as a "money pitcher," the guy you want on the mound to win the big games. It was his complete-game, two-hit shutout of the Toronto Blue Jays on the last day of the regular season in 1978—also Tiant's last game as a member of the Red Sox—that set up the team's one-game playoff the next day against the Yankees, for whom Tiant pitched a couple of seasons after leaving Boston. Tiant also won Game 1 of the 1975 American League Championship Series against the Oakland A's, and went on to win two games against the Cincinnati Reds in the World Series.

In the weeks following the Red Sox' World Series championship over the St. Louis Cardinals in the 2004 World Series, Tiant's name returned to the news on a couple of different occasions. One, when the team took a chance by signing, for short money, pitcher Wade Miller after the righthander had been non-tendered by the Houston Astros, more than a few people used Tiant as an example of the benefits of signing a once-successful pitcher making a comeback from an injury. In Miller's case, it was a frayed rotator cuff.

Tiant was also in the news when the Hall of Fame Veterans Committee mulled the fate of 25 former major leaguers who failed to gain induction during the years they were on the ballot that gets sent to voting members of the Baseball Writers Association of America. Tiant, whose career numbers are eerily similar to those of Hall of Fame pitcher Jim "Catfish" Hunter, was among the 25 players being considered.

Hunter's career record was 224-166, a .574 winning percentage. Tiant was 229-172, a .571 winning percentage. Hunter allowed 2,958 hits in 3,449⅓ innings. Tiant allowed 3,075 hits in 3,486⅓ innings. Hunter had 2,012 strikeouts and issued 954 walks. Tiant had 2,416 strikeouts and issued 1,104 walks.

This is a man who is not afraid to admit that, yes, he'd very much like to be enshrined in Cooperstown.

"I know what the numbers are," he said. "I'm very proud of what I did during my career. I'll always be proud of what I did."

Born in Marianao, Cuba, on November 23, 1940, Tiant was the son of Luis Tiant Sr., who pitched some 35 seasons in Cuba and in the old Negro Leagues. The highlight of Luis Jr.'s career occurred in 1975, when Fidel Castro allowed Tiant's parents to travel to the United States to watch their son start and win Game 1 of the World Series.

Tiant and his wife, Maria, live just outside Boston. They have three grown children, Luis, Isabel and Daniel.

Where Have You Gone?

JERRY CASALE

On April 15, 1959, a brawny, tough-talking kid from Brooklyn named Jerry Casale exploded into the big leagues. Making his first big-league start—he had made a couple of relief appearances late in the '58 season—Casale not only *pitched* the Red Sox to victory over the old Washington Senators, he provided offensive mite as well.

In winning his first major-league game, Casale also walloped a titanic three-run homer off Senators righthander Russ Kemmerer, himself a former Red Sox pitcher.

"The ball left the park right around over there," said Casale, pointing out toward the flag pole in left-center field during a visit to Fenway Park in September of 2004. "It was a shot. That might have been the happiest day of my career. I won the game. I hit that home run. I also struck out Roy Sievers three times. And he was a pretty good player.

"But do you know what *really* made me happy? It was a year earlier, when I put that big-league uniform on for the first time. To me, that's what did it. You're standing there, buttoning up that shirt, and you're looking in the mirror, and you're saying to yourself, 'I'm in the big leagues.' There's no other feeling like it in the world. God, they even gave me a locker next to Ted Williams. How could I ever forget all that?"

JERRY CASALE
Years with Red Sox: 1958-1960

Best Season with Red Sox: 1959

• Game: 31 • Record: 13-8 • ERA: 4.31 • Innings Pitched: 179⅔ •
• Hits Allowed: 162 • Strikeouts: 93 • Walks: 89 • Complete Games: 9 •

Though Casale posted a 13-8 record for the Red Sox in 1959, it was the best season of what turned out to be a vagabond career. By 1961 he was with the expansion Los Angeles Angels, in whose service he jump-started another chapter in Red Sox history by giving up Carl Yastrzemski's first major-league home run, and in '62 he closed out his own big-league career pitching for the Detroit Tigers.

Despite several outstanding seasons in the minors, Casale was only 17-24 as a big-league pitcher. But, oh, could he sock the ball: He hit three home runs in his rookie season, including the shot off Kemmerer, and on September 7, 1959, he teamed up with Don Buddin and Pumpsie Green to hit back-to-back-to-back home runs in a 12-4 victory over the Yankees at Fenway Park.

A gregarious, back-slapping, story-telling kind of guy, it seemed only natural that Jerry Joseph Casale, born in Brooklyn on September 27, 1933, would wind up in the restaurant business. He eventually bought a place on East 34th Street in New York called Pino's, where for nearly three decades the former pitcher served up great Italian dishes and even greater stories.

"I was in the meat business after I got out of baseball," he said. "I was living in New York, selling meat to different restaurants. And then a good friend of mine asked me if I wanted to take over this restaurant of his because he was retiring. I'm the kind of guy who can handle people well. I like meeting people, you know? And I figured you meet a lot of people running a restaurant, so I gave it a shot.

"The thing I missed most about baseball was the people. That baseball environment. And it's not a normal job, where you get up and go to work and do the same thing every day. And it turns out that running a restaurant is like baseball in that it's never the same from day to day, and you don't just go to work and sit there, like some people do."

Casale added a baseball theme to the place, including a mural of Fenway Park. Over the years a growing number of baseball people filled the place, including former Red Sox manager Joe Morgan, as well as Joe Castigleone, the longtime radio voice of the Red Sox.

"The food was excellent," said Castigleone. "He was his own chef at one time, and he knew what he was doing. And he'd love to come by your table and talk baseball. And at the slightest prompt, or even without one, he'd play this old tape recording he had of Phil Rizzuto broadcasting his home run off Bob Turley in '59. He loved that."

Casale also loved to send extravagant side dishes and hors d'oeuvres to his surprised diners, imploring them to try this or taste that. Happily, the diners would dig right in. Unhappily, they would discover the added treats had been added to their bill of fare.

Later in his career as a restaurateur, Casale went into business with former big-leaguers Art Shamsky and Ron Darling to open another Manhattan eatery, called Murray's. It failed. As for Pino's, it finally shut down in 2004.

Was Casale a bad businessman? Or, had his aging clientele simply moved on?

Casale has his own theory as to what happened with Pino's.

"We took a beating after 9-11," said Casale, referring to the September 11, 2001 terrorist attacks. "What happened that day was a terrible thing to a lot of people, but, on a business level, we lost a lot of our out-of-town customers, and we didn't bounce back from that real well. It knocked us out."

He and his wife, Margaret, to whom he was married in 1960, live in New Jersey. They have three grown children, Jimmy, Patty and Margaret. But even as he celebrated his 71st birthday, Jerry Casale, onetime slugging pitcher, onetime meat salesman, onetime restaurateur, was not ready to retire.

"I'm going crazy, trying to find a job so I can get back to work again," he said. "Plus, I'm getting old. It's a terrible thing to be old and out of work.

"I'm hoping to find a situation where they'll hire me to help bring people into the place. I have that know-how with people. Maybe there's a small place in New York that can use somebody like me. Hopefully I'll find that place and we'll all work together."

BRUCE HURST

I t's understandable that Bruce Hurst, as a kid growing up in St. George, Utah, had many a dream that centered around baseball.

You want to talk dreams? Surely this boy dreamed of playing in the big leagues. Surely he dreamed of starting a game in the World Series. And by the time he was a young man, Hurst realized both of these dreams.

But never in Hurst's wildest imagination—and never in his dreams— did he ever see himself standing on a baseball diamond in China, shar- ing his pitching knowledge with the eager young hurlers of the Chinese national team.

Yet it happened. After his big-league days ended in June of 1994, and after a couple of seasons as a pitching coach at the college and independ- ent minor-league levels, Hurst made a truly unique career decision when he went to work for Major League Baseball International.

Part ambassador of the game and part teacher, Hurst jumped into his new job with a passion. He conducted clinics in Italy, Germany, Amsterdam and the Czech Republic. A finesse pitcher during his own playing career, he taught his younger hurlers the secrets of the curve ball and the importance of changing speeds. And when language became a barrier, he simply used interpreters to get his point across.

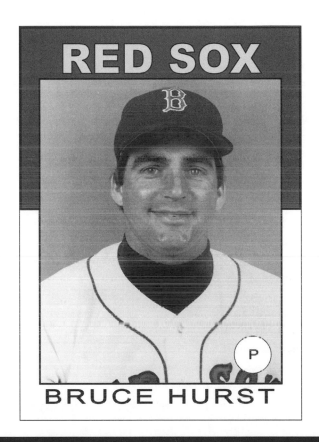

BRUCE HURST
Years with Red Sox: 1980-1988

Best Season with Red Sox: 1988 (5th in Cy Young voting)

• Games: 33 • Record: 18-6 • ERA: 3.66 • Innings Pitched: 216⅔ •
• Hits Allowed: 222 • Strikeouts: 166 • Walks: 65 • Complete Games: 7 •

In 2003 and '04, he was pitching coach of the Chinese National Team.

"The big thing was the language barrier," he said. "But when you have some pretty good translators there with you, you can do anything.

"There was an east vs. west mentality to a degree, as far as work ethic and what it takes to develop strength and mechanics and all that," he said. "There's a certain hurdle the Chinese pitchers invariably have to cross to get the most out of their arms. They understand our game very well. Logically, they get it. It's the physical part, and understanding how all the mechanics work, that's the challenge."

Hurst understands mechanics and pitching know-how as well as anyone. More than being just another pitching coach who talks a good game, Hurst's own teaching tools—again: patience, control, changing speeds—helped him post a 145-113 career record, including a 13-8 season in 1986 to help lead the Red Sox to a never-to-be-forgotten World Series against the New York Mets.

Much has been written about the Sox' inability to put the Mets away in Game 6, a collapse that culminated with Bill Buckner's historic mishandling of Mookie Wilson's grounder, which allowed the winning run to cross the plate and set the stage for the Mets' Series-clinching 8-5 victory over the Sox in Game 7. But had the collapse not occurred, Major League Baseball officials were already poised to announce the winner of the World Series MVP.

And that man was—that is, would have been—Bruce Hurst. He had dazzled the Mets in Game 1, throwing eight shutout innings in Boston's 1-0 victory. He came back in Game 5 and pitched the Sox to a 4-2 complete-game victory, putting his team on the brink of its first World Series championship since 1918.

But then came Game 6.

"I didn't find out until after the World Series that I had been named what I guess you could call the potential MVP," said Hurst. "And my reaction was at that time, and I mean this, that I was uneasy with it. I thought Marty (Barrett) and Spike (Owen) and Dave Henderson were huge in that World Series, and Marty had an incredible postseason all the way through. I don't know if my performance was that much better than what they had done."

Following the Sox' shocking loss in Game 6, the plan was that Oil Can Boyd would start the deciding Game 7 for the Red Sox. But when the game was pushed back a day because of rain, Red Sox manager John

McNamara made a fateful decision: He would, instead, come back with Hurst, on three days' rest, as his Game 7 starter.

And for most of the night, Hurst continued to befuddle the Mets; when he walked out to the mound in the bottom of the sixth inning at Shea Stadium, Boston held a 3-0 lead.

When the inning ended, the game was tied. Hurst was pinch-hit for in the seventh inning, and the Mets went on to an 8-5 victory, adding yet another sad chapter to Boston's quest for a World Series championship.

The key to the Mets' three-run rally in the bottom of the sixth was a two-run single to center by Keith Hernandez. To this day, Hurst regrets the pitch selection that led to Hernandez' hit.

"I wasn't 100 percent committed to throwing a fastball in that situation," he said. "I was thinking change-up or breaking ball. Looking back on it, I wish I had thrown something like that. I should have stepped off and maybe prepped myself a little bit, either made myself 100 percent committed to throwing that fastball or gone to another pitch."

Two years later, Hurst made another decision he wishes he could revisit. Coming off his career-best 18-6 season in 1988, Hurst filed for free agency in November, and a month later signed with the San Diego Padres, professing that he wanted his family to be closer to their home in Utah.

Hurst went on to have several good years with the Padres, but he never matched his 1988 numbers with the Red Sox. Moreover, his decision to leave the Red Sox removed him from Fenway Park, where, from 1986 to 1988, he was 33-9. His 56 victories at Fenway Park ranks him second only to Mel Parnell among lefthanders in the history of the old yard.

"If I had it to do all over again, all things considered, knowing what happened in San Diego, I probably should have stayed," Hurst said. "San Diego's a beautiful city, a great franchise, and I made a lot of good friends there, but I think Fenway was a good ballpark for me to pitch in."

When he's not circling the globe on behalf of Major League Baseball International, Hurst and his wife, Holly, live outside Phoenix. And while Hurst never did return to Boston, he did offer some words of encouragement when his Phoenix neighbor, Danny Ainge, decided to take over as director of basketball operations for the Boston Celtics.

"Yeah, I'm still doing what I'm doing," Hurst said. "Danny's the one who decided to get a real job."

BOB SMITH

Bob Smith had no way of knowing it at the time, but by 1960 the big-league portion of his career was over. The New Hampshire native had pitched parts of four seasons in the majors, including his 1955 debut with the Red Sox—which ended barely after it began—but by 1960 he was pitching for Denver in the American Association, with little hope of getting back to the big time.

One night, after a game against the Houston Buffs at Houston's Busch Stadium, Smith and some teammates stopped for a couple of beers at a bar across the street from the park. There, Smith met a nice young lady named Anita, a nurse at MD Anderson Hospital in Houston who was moonlighting as an usherette at Buffs games.

They dated, but you know how it goes. Smith was a ballplayer, with a season of baseball ahead of him—planes to catch, pitches to be thrown—and so the pitcher and the nurse drifted apart, their romance nothing more than a summertime fling. Sounds like a Top 40 song from the 60s, no?

By 1984, Bob Smith was in the paper business, working for Great Northern Nekoosa Corporation. A business trip landed him in Houston, and Smith, after a day's work and a little after-hours leisure time on his hands, got to wondering whatever became of the lovely

BOB SMITH
Year with Red Sox: 1955

Best Season with Red Sox: 1955

• Games: 1 • Record: 0-0 • ERA: 0.00 • Innings Pitched: 1⅔ •
• Hits Allowed: 1 • Strikeouts: 1 • Walks: 1 • Saves: 0 •

Anita. Sitting in his hotel room with not much else to do, and overcome with curiosity, he looked her up in the local phone book, and, to his surprise, found a name and a number.

He picked up the phone and pressed the buttons.

"I don't know if you remember me," he started to say, and Anita, thinking it over for a moment, offered that, yes, yes, um, sort of, she did remember a Bob Smith. Baseball player, right? They talked for a while, and then Smith, by now twice divorced, asked Anita if they'd like to meet. A cup of coffee, perhaps. Maybe dinner.

Now Anita remembered the name, remembered the voice, even remembered Bob Smith as being a good-looking fellow. What she had no way of knowing was how well the old ballplayer had held up over the years, and she wasn't taking any chances: When the doorbell rang, she was going to look through the peephole first, take a good long look, and then look again, and then decide whether she'd undo the latch.

The doorbell rang. Anita took a look. She did not need that second look. She opened the door.

"I liked what I saw," said Anita.

Today, Bob and Anita Smith, happily married, are living in retirement in Aiken, South Carolina.

The lesson to be learned here?

"My advice to all the young ladies is to keep your phone number listed over the years," said Smith. "You never know what's going to happen."

Smith admits it's a rather offbeat story, but he never tires of telling it again. And considering his own playing career never reached the heights he had envisioned for himself when he signed his first contract with the Red Sox, the silver lining is that, as his career was at its end, he was able to meet the woman who would become his life partner. It's just that it took him almost 25 years to figure it all out.

"I never forgot her," said Smith. "She was the best-looking young nurse in Houston. She was tall, with a nice figure, and this attractive beehive hairdo. And when I met her again after all those years, she still looked great."

Anita's take on this was that " . . . I couldn't believe he had such a great memory after all that time. I couldn't believe he was available. And I couldn't believe that *I* was available at the time. I guess it was just meant to be."

Robert Gilchrist Smith was born on February 1, 1931, in Woodsville, New Hampshire. A high school baseball star in New Hampshire, he signed with the Red Sox in 1948, but lost three seasons while serving in the Army in the early '50s. He mostly played baseball during his Army days, teaming up with, among many others, future big-league pitcher (and later big-league manager) Roger Craig.

"I probably pitched as much on that Army team as I would have had I been in the minors," said Smith. "So when I left the Army and was ready to play professional baseball again, it's not like I lost a whole lot."

His Army tour ended in 1953. In 1954, he was back in the minors. On April 29, 1955, he made his major-league debut for the Red Sox, working one and two-thirds innings of shutout relief against the Chicago White Sox at Comiskey Park.

But Smith was soon back in the minors, pitching for the Sox' Louisville farm club. He was an early cut in spring training in 1956, and landed with the Sox' new top farm club, the San Francisco Seals. He was then drafted by the St. Louis Cardinals, for whom he appeared in six games in 1957 before being sold to the Pittsburgh Pirates early in the

Photo courtesy of Bob and Anita Smith

season. He spent most of the next three seasons with the Pirates, usually working out of the bullpen, and in June, 1959, he was claimed off the waiver wire by the Detroit Tigers.

He appeared in nine games for the Tigers, appearing in his last big-league game on September 23, 1959, against the Kansas City Athletics.

And then came 1960, and the minor leagues, and a trip to Houston.

And a decision to pick up the phone and call Anita.

After that 1960 date, Anita went on to become an usherette at Astros games when big-league baseball finally landed in Houston. That was the closest she came to the majors until 1984, when the telephone rang.

Where Have You Gone?

JEFF PLYMPTON

The 2003-04 winter made for a busy, bustling off-season for the Red Sox. They hired a new manager, Terry Francona. They acquired one of the game's best starting pitchers in Curt Schilling, and one of its best closers in Keith Foulke.

They tried, and failed, to swing a blockbuster deal that would have brought Alex Rodriguez to Boston for Manny Ramirez.

But the Red Sox were doing more than moving players. They were also moving furniture. As part of the seemingly never-ending renovation of ancient Fenway Park, the Red Sox closed down and gutted a bowling alley that had long operated in the basement of the old ballyard, opting to use the space for the team's executive offices.

When it came time to cart everything downstairs, the Red Sox enlisted the help of a local company, ABC Moving Services of nearby Somerville.

The Red Sox knew they could count on the folks from ABC. What they didn't know was that one of those folks would be a former pitcher of theirs.

Jeff Plympton, a Massachusetts native and onetime University of Maine standout who appeared in four games for the Red Sox in 1991, was, by the winter of 2003-04, working as an account representative for

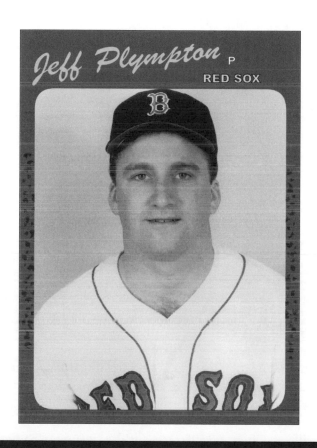

JEFF PLYMPTON
Year with Red Sox: 1991

Best Season with Red Sox: 1991

• Games: 4 • Record: 0-0 • ERA: 0.00 • Innings Pitched 5⅓ •
• Hits Allowed: 5 • Strikeouts: 2 • Walks: 4 • Saves: 0 •

ABC Moving Services, one of those smallish companies that prides itself in delivering quality service and sending out account reps who have good people skills. So here's Jeff Plympton, a pleasant, amiable guy, working in the moving business, his baseball days far, far in his past, and all of a sudden he's being assigned to work in the very building that provided some of the biggest thrills of his life.

The Red Sox had a game plan: They wanted to lug their baseball operations department down to the space once occupied by the late, great Ryan Family Amusement Center, the official name for the famed basement bowling alley. And Plympton was being called in for a different kind of save opportunity.

Picture yourself as Jeff Plympton. In 1991, you're pitching for the Red Sox. Twelve years later, you're pitching in as the team moves its furniture downstairs.

"People ask me if was weird, and, well, *of course* it was weird," said Plympton. "I walked into (general manager) Theo Epstein's office, and right there, on the wall, were all the placement charts showing which teams all the minor-leaguers were on.

"I can remember seeing those same placement charts when I was playing," he said. "I remember coming in to see Ed Kenney, who was the farm director at the time, and, like all of us of in the minors, trying to get a few extra bucks before heading to spring training, or maybe some extra meal money. I saw my name up there on the wall and hoped there'd come a day when they'd move it over to the big-league side."

Plympton resisted the temptation to rummage through the file cabinets in search of whatever aging, crinkly scouting reports still existed containing his name. Instead, he simply did his job, getting the necessary paperwork done for ABC. The move from upstairs to downstairs went by without a hitch, and within a few days Plympton had moved on to a new assignment.

"But I took one last look up at that wall before I left," he said. "I looked at all the names. You know, most of them won't make the big leagues. That's just the way it is. When you're in the minor leagues, that's life. But all those kids—all those names—they still have the dream. You have to admire them for that. They were on their way to spring training with all their dreams."

Plympton's dream began in 1987, when he was selected by the Red Sox in the 10th round of the June amateur draft. He had played baseball at King Phillip Regional High School in nearby Wrentham, and later became a standout for the University of Maine Black Bears, appearing in the 1986 College World Series.

Mostly a relief pitcher in the minors, he made it to the majors for four games in 1991, making his debut in the ninth inning of a June 15 day game against the California Angels at Fenway Park. Pitching in relief of Wes Gardner, he worked a scoreless inning to wrap up a 13-3 Boston victory.

He pitched in three other games, totaling five and one-third innings. He didn't allow a run. His last appearance of the season—and, as things happened, his big-league career—was on September 19, 1991, a 9-2 loss to the Baltimore Orioles at Fenway Park. He worked the final two innings of the blowout, getting the last batter he faced, Mike Devereaux, on a fly to center.

You probably already know the rest of the story. He landed back in the minors, and then came the injuries, followed by the ravages of time and a never-ending flow of younger players. After one too many seasons on the minor-league side of that wall chart in then-general manager Dan Duquette's office, Plympton retired from baseball.

He and his wife, Linda, remained in the Boston area. They have two children, Nicole and Jeffrey. Occasionally, Jeffrey will bounce into the house with a collection of friends, whereupon the boy will proudly slide a tape into the VCR to prove that, yes, absolutely, his dad *did* pitch for the Red Sox.

In the fall of 2004, Jeff Plympton left ABC Moving to begin a new career as recreation director of the town of Wrentham. With the town having just acquired an 80-acre parcel of land from a former state school, with plans to develop the property into athletic fields, Plympton looked forward to the new venture.

"I can't say it'll be as exciting as pitching for the Red Sox," Plympton said, "but I'm looking forward to this new career. Part of my job is to help raise the $5 million we'll need to get the job done. But I like the challenge of it all."

Where Have You Gone?

JOHN KENNEDY

By the time John Kennedy joined the Red Sox, in 1970, he was already in his eighth season in the big leagues. And though he had had his shot at being an everyday player, now he was both a journeyman and a backup, thankful for whatever opportunities came his way.

So anonymous was this newest member of the Red Sox that, when he came to bat for the first time, most of the crowd at Fenway Park didn't even know he was on the team.

A week and a half earlier, on June 26, 1970, the Red Sox purchased Kennedy's contract from the Milwaukee Brewers. At the time the Brewers made the deal, Kennedy was idling in the minor leagues. Having joined the Red Sox, he went directly to the bench . . . until the bottom of the fifth inning of the Sox' Saturday matinee against the Cleveland Indians on July 5, 1970.

With the Sox trailing 3-2, Red Sox manager Eddie Kasko dusted off his new utility player as a pinch-hitter for starting pitcher Mike Nagy. Pitching for the Indians was rookie lefthander Rick Austin, a 23-year-old who had made his big-league debut just a couple of weeks earlier.

Now, before getting to what Kennedy accomplished in his first at-bat with the Red Sox, the tape must be rewound four months, to spring training. Both the Indians and the Milwaukee Brewers were holding

BOSTON RED SOX

JOHN
KENNEDY   INFIELD

JOHN KENNEDY
Years with Red Sox: 1970-1974

Best Season with Red Sox: 1971

• Games: 74 • Batting Average: .276 • At Bats: 272 • Hits: 75 •
• Runs: 41 • Home Runs: 5 • RBIs: 22 • Slugging Percentage: .412 •

spring training in Arizona at the time, and the two teams frequently played each other. And it so happened that, during spring training, the right-handed-hitting Kennedy was making some adjustments in his swing, trying to dump the ball the other way rather than pull it to left.

Here now was Kennedy, making his debut with the Red Sox, and here were the Indians, who knew exactly what the guy was going to try to do. Remember, they had seen a lot of the guy during the carefree days of the Cactus League. So they moved their right fielder, Roy Foster, into shallow territory.

"And I could see that," said Kennedy. "And I'm thinking that if I get an outside pitch and take it the other way, I might be able to hit it over his head. I was at that point in my career where I had to think a little harder, and hustle, play the game right, which I always tried to do, if I wanted to stay around."

Kennedy got his outside pitch. He sliced a liner to right. The ball sailed over the head of a leaping Foster, and then hugged the fence in the right-field corner and rolled out toward the bullpens, some 380 feet from home plate. As Foster and center fielder Vada Pinson chased after the ball, Kennedy, gasping for air, chugged around the bases. As he was rounding second, he noticed that third-base coach Eddie Popowski was waving him home—this in spite of the fact that nobody was out.

Kennedy kept running, registering an inside-the-park home run. The Red Sox would score two more runs in the inning en route to an 8-4 victory over the Indians.

After the game, Popowski, a baseball lifer whose career dated back to the 1930s when he played for the old "House of David" barnstorming team, approached Kennedy with a smile and a quip.

"If that had been Yastrzemski or Petrocelli, I would have put up the take sign," said Pop. "But when I saw it was only you, I said, 'What the hell.'"

It was not the most historic hit of Kennedy's career — as a rookie with the Washington Senators in 1962, he homered in his first major-league at-bat—but the veteran's hustle and intuition had made a strong impression on the Red Sox. He wound up playing parts of five seasons with the club, and in 1971 the generally light-hitting infielder came to the plate 272 times and hit a career-high .276.

Kennedy, who was born in Chicago on May 29, 1941, also found a permanent home in the Boston area.

"I had played in the minor leagues with Mike Hegan, and his wife and my wife were friends," said Kennedy. "They were always saying how great it was to live in Boston."

What's funny about all this is that Hegan, whose family was from just outside Boston in the city of Lynn, wound up settling in Milwaukee, which isn't far from Kennedy's hometown of Chicago. And Kennedy settled in the Boston area, not far from Hegan Country.

Kennedy's career ended in 1974—his name last appears in a big-league boxscore on June 16, 1974 as a ninth-inning defensive replacement against the California Angels—but the Red Sox had yet more plans for him: They re-hired him as a minor-league manager. He managed Single-A Winston-Salem in 1975, followed by two seasons with Double-A Bristol. He moved on to manage or coach at the minor-league level for the Oakland A's and New York Yankees, and then left baseball for a couple of years when he accepted a job back working in the abandoned property department of the Massachusetts treasurer's office.

Abandoned property was fun for a couple of years, but Kennedy decided that newer property was the way to go: He returned to baseball as a scout for the Philadelphia Phillies, and later served in a similar capacity for the Yankees and Tigers.

In 2003, Kennedy returned to field duty as manager of the North Shore Spirit of the independent Northeast League. He was named the league's Manager of the Year in '03 after leading the Spirit to the North Division championship. He rounded out his coaching staff with former Red Sox players Rich Gedman and Dick Radatz. The team plays its home games at Lynn's Fraser Field, the very place where Mike Hegan's father, Jim Hegan, honed his skills before embarking on a 17-year big-league playing career.

Kennedy and his wife, Betty, live in Peabody, Massachusetts. They have two children, Scott, born in 1964, and Kristen, born in 1968. When he's not managing the Spirit, and when he's in the spirit, Kennedy makes occasional appearances as a baseball expert on various Boston television stations.

Where Have You Gone?

JIM PAGLIARONI

The accident happened on a weekday in March of 1997. And it was, until the moment of impact, a typical day for Jim Pagliaroni, meaning that he was a man on the move, with meetings to attend, phone calls to return, deals to make.

Only now he was stopped in morning traffic on I-80 just outside of Sacramento. As he sat there in the chaos of his morning commute, waiting for the traffic to clear, he heard a noise, and then, just as he was registering the sound he was hearing, his car seemed to collapse and cave in all at once and all around him.

He had been hit from behind by another vehicle that was later said to be traveling in excess of 70 mph as it hurtled down an on-ramp into the awaiting traffic.

"I woke up in the ambulance," Pagliaroni recalled. "They were cutting my clothes off me."

Pagliaroni suffered a broken back, cracked ribs, a fractured skull and severe facial injuries.

That's the bad news.

The good news, if that's how one chooses to seek out the sunny side of a life-threatening car wreck, is that Jim Pagliaroni, forever a man on

JIM PAGLIARONI
Years with Red Sox: 1955-1961

Best Season with Red Sox: 1961

• Games: 120 • Batting Average: .242 • At Bats: 376 • Hits: 91 •
• Runs: 50 • Home Runs: 16 • RBIs: 58 • Slugging Percentage: .415 •

the go, had finally reached a moment of clarity in his life. Suddenly, the next deal, the next plane flight, didn't seem so important.

"I've never had a fear of dying," he said. "But I knew that day I was fortunate to be alive. Heck, my head was split open like a grape. My wife had seen my car after the accident, and she said, 'OK, that's enough of this. You're going to slow down and enjoy life.'"

A onetime "bonus baby" who made his big-league debut with the Red Sox in 1955, Pagliaroni never emerged as one of the game's great stars. But he did enjoy an 11-year career in the big leagues, after which he made a graceful transition into the business world.

He had been preparing for this life after baseball. When he was a young catcher with the Red Sox, Ted Williams told him, "Don't ever forget that baseball is just a means to an end." Knowing, then, that there'd be many, many years of life after baseball, and learning to appreciate the business end of things during his years as a player rep with the Pittsburgh Pirates, he looked ahead.

While still playing, he and his father-in-law, Bill Miller, opened a small family-style restaurant. Later, they landed an A&W Root Beer fast-food franchise.

"But I wanted more," he said. "I had good people skills, and I enjoyed the world of sales. You have to have an aptitude for it, and that was me. And, really, it wasn't about the money. I know people say that kind of thing all the time, but for me it was all about the chase. It was about the accomplishment. It was like a team thing, playing baseball, reaching goals, making things happen."

So he branched out. He interviewed for a sales job with Sacramento-based Monarch Foods, which led to a job with Dolphin Seafoods, which was owned by Unilever, the world's largest consumer products company. He eventually landed with Ragu (the pasta sauce people), also owned by Unilever, emerging as sales manager of the western United States.

He continued to branch out. He headed up the marketing division of a kosher pickle company. At the time of the accident, he was doing consulting work for a national bakery business.

"I realized, that day, that there must be a better way of doing things," he said. "And I resolved that, from that day on, I would make changes in my life."

Instead of chasing after the next deal, Pagliaroni chose to immerse himself in activities that brought joy to his life, yet also stimulated him intellectually. The result was a business called Market Solutions, based in

Sacramento, which Pagliaroni jointly owns with Bill Ludwig, the former CEO of the Rice Growers Association of California.

"We work with companies in the food and agricultural business that want to restructure their sales and marketing," he said. "That's about as simple as I can make it."

To some, it still sounds like "work." Only to Pagliaroni, who grew up poor in Long Beach, California, it's a chance to get away from non-stop selling and to instead use his years of experience to help fix other companies.

"I was playing baseball when Marvin Miller was running the Players Association, and a lot happened during that time," Pagliaroni said. "That's what really opened my eyes to the business side of things. With what I'm doing know, I still get to work in business without the pressure of sales. I'm always going to be a Type A producer, only now I'm busy through consulting."

Pagliaroni, a busy adult, was also a busy teenager. He was just 17 when he signed with the Red Sox in 1955, appearing in his first big-league game on August 13. In his lone plate appearance, he drove in a run with a sacrifice fly.

The next year, he was even busier: In June of 1956, he married his high school sweetheart, and he and Linda have been together ever since. They have two grown daughters, Laura and Dana, and four grandchildren.

After idling on the Boston bench as a "bonus baby," Pagliaroni didn't return to the big leagues until 1960. He hit 16 home runs for the Sox in 1961 and remained with the team through 1962, and then was traded to the Pirates.

The highlight of his career took place on May 8, 1968, when, while playing for the Oakland A's, he caught Jim "Catfish" Hunter's 4-0 perfect game against the Minnesota Twins.

Three days later, with the A's hosting the White Sox on NBC's "Game of the Week," team owner Charles O. Finley sought to capitalize on the perfect game by presenting a $5,000 bonus to Hunter on national television. Hunter, knowing the penny-pinching owner was after a publicity grab, told Finley he wouldn't do it unless his catcher also received a bonus.

"Jim was a pretty good businessman himself," said Pagliaroni. "I wound up getting $1,500. Finley was livid."

Where Have You Gone?

TOMMY HARPER

There was a time, and it wasn't long ago, when it was understood that Tommy Harper would never step inside Fenway Park again. He had been fired from his job as a coach, and Harper did go gently into that good hardball night: He sued the Red Sox for racial discrimination. And the Red Sox settled.

But while Harper will never forget the way he was treated by the Red Sox of the early '80s, he *forgave* them. He eventually returned to the team as a coach, and, like all coaches, worked hard to survive the various regime changes that are so common in big-league baseball. So when new manager Terry Francona brought in a mostly new coaching staff in 2004, Harper felt comfortable taking a job as a minor-league instructor.

"But I'm always careful what I say about the Red Sox, because if I say something that's construed as negative, people are just going to say, 'Oh, he's a bitter guy,'" he said. "Well, I'll tell you this: I have never been bitter about anything with the Red Sox. Never, never. They settled with me. They gave me the settlement I deserved, and we all went on with our lives. You want to talk about bitter? Man, I wouldn't be able to survive if I were a bitter man. It wouldn't sit well with me.

TOMMY HARPER
Years with Red Sox: 1972-1974

Best Season with Red Sox: 1973

• Games: 147 • Batting Average: .281 • At Bats: 566 • Hits: 159 •
• Runs: 92 • Home Runs: 17 • RBIs: 71 • Stolen Bases: 54 •

"I'm not going to let anybody or anything change my attitude toward life. So when I give somebody an answer, it's the way I feel—and not because I'm disgruntled."

Besides, if anyone *does* put it out there that Harper is "disgruntled," he has a quick comeback.

"Well, the courts found in my favor," he said. "So that's proof that I wasn't just a disgruntled ex-employee."

But while Harper wants to continue his relationship with the Red Sox, now owned by a group headed up by John W. Henry, Tom Werner and team president Larry Lucchino, he has no problem speaking his mind when he sees the need. Age, after all, can be liberating, and Harper, though he still has a teenager's body, turned 64 in October of 2004. And anyway, it's easier to clear your chest when you've already been shown to be in the right in exposing some of the leftover elements of the Red Sox' troubled history in the area of race relations.

"I don't know these people," he said, referring to the new owners of the Red Sox, "so I need to reserve my judgment. I need some time to see what they're all about. I haven't made up my mind about them yet. But have there been improvements? Yes. If you looked at it objectively, any-one would have to say it's better."

Harper often is asked if it is his dream to see an African-American manage the Red Sox. This, after all, is a man who knows well the racial history of the Red Sox. He knows about the 1945 sham tryout in which Negro League stars Jackie Robinson, Sam Jethroe and Marvin Williams were paraded out to the Fenway Park diamond and then never again contacted. He knows that the Red Sox were the last team to have a African-American player on their big-league roster. (Pumpsie Green, 1959.) He knows that for too many years the club employed executives and coaches who had little or no interest in black players.

"It's not my *dream* to see a black man as manager of the Red Sox," he said. "It doesn't have to be a black man managing here. What I'd like to see is the *opportunity* for a black man to manage here, and I don't think the Red Sox have worked to make that happen yet. I haven't seen it.

"I know they've interviewed black men for the job," he said. "But were they serious about it? That's what I'm not sure about."

Tommy Harper was born on October 14, 1940 in Oak Grove, Louisiana, but grew up in Alameda, California. He was signed by the Cincinnati Reds in 1960, and made his major-league debut in 1962. He was one of the game's top base stealers over the next decade—including the 1969 season with the Seattle Pilots, for whom he stole a league-leading 73 bases—and when he joined the Red Sox in 1972 he instantly became one of the fastest runners this historically lead-footed franchise had ever seen. He stole 54 bases for the Red Sox in 1973, which was still a club record more than 30 years later.

For years and years, a conga line of dimwits advanced the notion that, from 1939 to 1990, only four men played regularly in left field for the Red Sox: Ted Williams, Carl Yastrzemski, Jim Rice and Mike Greenwell. It's nonsense, of course, as it leaves out the fact that Williams actually played right field his first season with the Red Sox, along with conveniently omitting the seasons Williams was serving his country in the military.

And, yes, the left field myth omits Tommy Harper, who took over left field in 1973 when Yastrzemski moved to first base. But Harper doesn't mind the slight: "It was one of my better seasons," he said.

Harper's career ended with the Baltimore Orioles in 1976. His first stint as a coach with the Red Sox lasted from 1980 to 1984, with Harper getting the gate after exposing the fact that for many years the team had tolerated a practice in which a segregated Elks Club in Winter Haven, Florida, had issued guest passes to white players and members of the media during spring training—omitting players of color. For whatever reasons, Harper was fired at the end of the '84 season. He sued. With the Massachusetts Commission Against Discrimination championing his cause, Harper eventually negotiated a settlement with the Red Sox. He returned to the club in 2000.

Harper and his wife, Bonnie Jean, still live in the Boston area.

Where Have You Gone?

MEL PARNELL

His aching left elbow serving as his agent, advisor and confidante, Mel Parnell decided it was time to stop pitching and perhaps seek out another way to be a part of the game he loved—and still loves—so very much.

Managing, he thought, might be the way to go. So Parnell returned to his hometown and skippered the minor-league New Orleans Pelicans in 1959, followed by stops with the Alpine Cowboys, the York White Roses and, finally, the Seattle Rainiers of the Pacific Coast League.

But as much as Parnell loved baseball, especially during the years in which he emerged as the best lefthander the Red Sox had seen since the days of George Herman Ruth, he discovered, to his sorrow, that managing wasn't as much fun as pitching.

"Managing made for too many headaches," he said. "Even back then, you had to cope with too many problems. To me, it took away from the baseball thought process. I thought managing meant all you thought about was baseball. Instead, I found myself worrying about all kinds of things that had nothing to do with baseball. Managers have to worry about too much off-the-field stuff. I just wanted to worry about the on-the-field stuff."

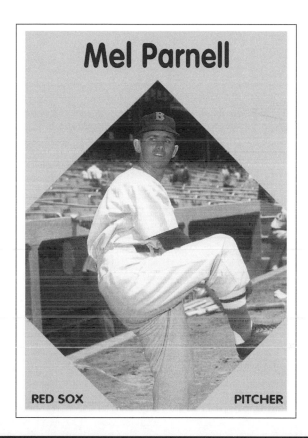

MEL PARNELL
Years with Red Sox: 1947-1956

Best Season with Red Sox: 1949 (All Star, 4th in MVP Voting)

• Games: 39 • Record: 25-7 • ERA: 2.77 • Innings Pitched: 295⅓ •
• Hits Allowed: 258 • Strikeouts: 122 • Walks: 134 • Complete Games: 27 •

Convinced that managing was not for him, Parnell and his wife, Delma, returned home to New Orleans.

And what did he decide to do with the rest of his life? Turns out the man who did not enjoy managing minor-league baseball players went into the pest control business.

Is there a connection? Minor-league baseball players and pests?

"No, no connection," he said. "It's just something I wandered into and did well with. I started the business from scratch. I had been in the automobile business for a while, but there was a market for pest control in New Orleans.

"There was a termite problem in New Orleans," Parnell said. "It was a real problem. There was a breed of termite that was brought in from Formosa and it spread from here. It was just eating everything up."

But Parnell wasn't completely divorced from baseball. Though he had made a decision not to pursue a career in baseball, Parnell had been approached by Gurt Gowdy, then the play-by-play voice of the Red Sox on television and radio, to take a shot at the broadcast booth. And why not? Parnell had been a big star during his playing days, and he had a pleasant, soothing personality Gowdy thought might work well in front of a microphone.

At first, Parnell thought the broadcasting gig would be a lark, something to do for a year or two before re-settling in New Orleans. But teaming up with some of the best broadcasters ever to work in Boston—in addition to Gowdy, he sat alongside Ned Martin and Ken Coleman—Parnell became a mainstay of Boston's baseball waves, carving out a 10-year career.

"The best year, obviously, was 1967, the 'Impossible Dream' year," he said. "I have so many memories of that season. The Red Sox just came out of nowhere. So many thrills.

"But I was also working the night Tony Conigliaro got beaned," he said, referring to the August night when California Angels pitcher Jack Hamilton threw a pitch that hit the Red Sox right fielder in the left eye, a tragedy that shortened what could have been a Hall of Fame career.

"That's one I'll never forget," he said. "To be on the air when that happened . . . it was just terrible. But I said then, and I'll say it now, that I don't believe Hamilton was throwing at Tony. No way. Tony was a real aggressive hitter, and he liked to lean way out over the plate."

Melvin Lloyd Parnell was born on June 13, 1922, in New Orleans. He was just a few weeks shy of his 25th birthday when he made his major-league debut with the Red Sox in 1947, but it was in 1948 that the kid known then as "Dusty" emerged as one of the game's best young lefthanders. He went 15-8 in '48, and a year later he submitted one of the finest seasons in Red Sox history, going 25-7 with a 2.77 ERA.

Playing on a team better known for its offensive stars, led by Ted Williams but including the likes of Bobby Doerr, Johnny Pesky and, later, Jackie Jensen and Jimmy Piersall, Parnell was a *pitching* star. During a six-year stretch from 1948 through 1953, he was 109-56.

He also threw a no-hitter during his days with the Red Sox, beating the Chicago White 4-0 on July 14, 1956. At the time, it was the first no-hitter by a Red Sox pitcher in 33 years.

"I've read stories about pitchers who said they didn't really know when they had a no-hitter going," Parnell said. "That's all baloney. Trust me, they knew. I always knew. And I sure knew that day. Heck, Jensen came up to me and said, 'Make sure they don't hit the ball at me. I'll blow it.'"

But in some ways Parnell is also famous for a game in which he did *not* pitch.

On October 4, 1948, Red Sox manager Joe McCarthy chose journeyman righty Denny Galehouse to start a one-game playoff against the Cleveland Indians to determine the American League pennant winner, and, hence, the AL's representative in the World Series. Galehouse didn't get out of the fourth inning; the Red Sox lost, 8-3. And ever since, critics have argued that either Parnell, who would have been working on three days' rest, or Ellis Kinder should have been given the starting assignment.

"I thought I was going to pitch that game," said Parnell. "When I got to the park, Mr. McCarthy told me he was going with (Galehouse). And that was that."

Did he complain?

"You didn't complain to Joe McCarthy," said Parnell. "He was the manager. It was his decision."

And, ultimately, that's why Mel Parnell went into pest control: He was old school, a pitcher who believed you never questioned a manager's decision. So when minor-leaguers questioned *his* decisions, he happily went home to New Orleans.

Where Have You Gone?

FRANK SULLIVAN

L ooking back on the end of his sometimes brilliant but often over-
looked major-league pitching career, Frank Sullivan put it this way:
"I was 33 years old, with no job, no prospects and no money."

The question, then, is this: When you're 33 years old, and you've just
lost your job, and there's nothing on the horizon in the way of a second
career, and you're short on dough, what *do* you do with your life?

In Frank Sullivan's case, the decision was easy: You stuff as much of
your personal effects as will fit into a couple of suitcases, and you move
halfway across the world to a place you've never before so much as visited.

The place was Lihue, on the island of Kauai, in the young state of
Hawaii. Hey, sometimes aging pitchers get picked up by expansion
teams. Sullivan, who had more on his mind than baseball, chose to sign
on with an expansion *state*.

"I played most of my baseball in the '50s, and back then you didn't
make a whole lot of money doing it," said Sullivan, who made his major-
league debut with the Red Sox on July 31, 1953. "I think the most I ever
made in a season was $25,000, which was fine back then, but it's not
enough money to live on for the rest of your life. And I think like a lot

FRANK SULLIVAN
Years with Red Sox: 1953-1960

Best Season with Red Sox: 1955 (All Star)

• Games: 35 • Record: 18-13 • ERA: 2.91 • Innings Pitched: 260 •
• Hits Allowed: 235 • Strikeouts: 129 • Walks: 100 • Complete Games: 16 •

of players back then, I didn't really have a plan for what I'd be doing with my life *after* baseball.

"And I didn't want to be digging ditches in front of people who knew me, or people who had been cheering for me just a few years earlier. So I took off."

Understand that to some degree Sullivan is winking at you as he speaks those words. For while he was by no means wealthy when he played his last game in the big leagues, he wasn't broke. The truth is that he had about $5,000 in the bank when he made way for Hawaii, surely not enough to enable a guy to snub his nose at the time clock, but sufficient seed money, at least in those days, to get started in a new career.

Besides, it wasn't digging ditches in front of old friends that worried Sullivan; after all, sturdy, blue-collar work had dotted his resume for much of his life. This is a man who once moved to Maine to help run a repair dock for sailboats, and who made a little side money by sailing boats belonging to their too-busy owners down south during the off season.

It was in keeping with his lifestyle, then, that he'd go to Hawaii and then go to work. Even if it meant digging ditches. And he didn't go alone. Sammy White, his old catcher during their days together on the Red Sox, also chose to go on a midlife adventure to a strange new place. (White, who played nine of his eleven big-league seasons with the Red Sox, was living in Hawaii when he died in 1991.)

Sullivan's first work in Hawaii was helping run a beach at a hotel, a job he landed thanks to his then-girlfriend and future wife, Marilyn, who worked at the hotel as an executive secretary. But it was Hawaii's *other* recreational pastime—golf—that became Sullivan's post-baseball career. He took a job at a local golf course as a way to make ends meet, but he wound up becoming general manager of the place. He ran golf courses on Kauai for more than 35 years, and as of 2004 he was still doing part-time work for the Grove Farm Company, which owns, among many other interests, the Puakea Golf Course.

"I live on a small island and have five golf courses within a mile of my house and the weather is always great," said Sullivan. "I guess I'm doing OK."

Franklin Leal Sullivan was born on January 23, 1930, in Hollywood, California. He signed with the Red Sox in 1948, made it to Fenway in '53, and then had a five-year run in which he was one of the game's best pitchers. He won 74 games from 1954 to 1958, including an 18-13 record for the 1955 Red Sox. He worked three shutout innings in the 1955 All-Star Game at Milwaukee's County Stadium as the Midsummer Classic hummed into extra innings, and then was taken out of the yard and into the history books when the St. Louis Cardinals' Stan Musial led off the 12th inning with a game-winning home run.

He remained with the Red Sox through 1960, but his record slipped to 6-16. Traded to the Phillies for pitcher Gene Conley, Sullivan was 3-16 in 1961, meaning that over a two-year period he was 9-32. Released by the Phillies in 1962, Sullivan was picked up by the Minnesota Twins, for whom he spent parts of two seasons working out of the bullpen.

It was after being released by the Twins in 1963 that Sullivan uttered one of the most famous quotes in baseball history: "I am in the twilight of a mediocre career," he said. Though other players in baseball and in other sports—indeed, in other professions—have used that line many times over the years, Sullivan is credited with saying it first. Do a Google search, using "Frank Sullivan," "twilight" and "career" as your key words, and you'll see that, as Sullivan is enjoying retirement on Kauai, his famous quote is still hard at work in cyberspace.

Frank and Marilyn Sullivan continue to live on Kauai, though they grudgingly make occasional trips back to the mainland.

"That airline crap is brutal," he said. "I'd rather have a root canal than put one foot on an airplane."

They have a son, Mike, and a granddaughter, Kea, who occasionally gets picked up after school by her grandfather, who sounds like a man who's never in a hurry to get anywhere.

Where Have You Gone?

GENE MICHAEL

If you consider yourself a hardened, seasoned, wise-to-the-ways-of-the world Red Sox fan, chances are that you are surprised, but not shocked, to find Gene Michael's name in this book.

And if you're merely a fan on the fringes of Red Sox Nation, an observer without the obsessiveness, you're either saying, "Gene Michael never played for the Red Sox," or, "Who is Gene Michael?"

Most baseball fans are aware that Gene "Stick" Michael is a one-time big-league utility infielder who spent most of his career with the Yankees and who, in 1973, played a significant role in one of the biggest Red Sox-Yankees brawls in history. And, yes, most fans also recognize Michael as a former big-league manager, general manager and scout.

OK, now for the tricky part. Did Gene Michael, as we are claiming, really play for the Red Sox?

Well, yes. And no. It all depends on your definition of the word "played."

What is undeniable is that on February 15, 1976, just as spring training was getting underway, the Red Sox signed Michael to a contract. He was a few months shy of his 38th birthday, a veteran of 10 seasons in the big leagues, seven of them with the Yankees, and the Red Sox were hop-

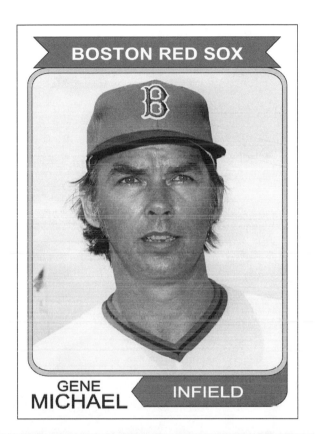

BOSTON RED SOX

GENE
MICHAEL

INFIELD

GENE MICHAEL
Years with Red Sox: 1976

No game action

ing he'd be a steady backup infielder on a team that already had young Rick Burleson at shortstop and veteran Denny Doyle at second.

What is also undeniable is that Michael earned a spot on the team's 25-man roster and was in uniform on Opening Day, a 1-0 loss to the Baltimore Orioles at Memorial Stadium.

But what happened during the first month of the 1976 season is all you really need to know to understand the old, ornery rivalry that is the Red Sox vs. the Yankees. Day after day, game after game, Michael sat on the bench for the Red Sox. He never got an at-bat. He never pinch-ran. He didn't even serve as a late-inning defensive replacement, which presumably was the reason he was signed in the first place.

"They brought me in to break all of Ted Williams's records, and then they didn't play me," said Michael. "If they had given me a chance, that might be my number out there in right field, next to Ted's."

Perhaps Red Sox manager Darrell Johnson could have found a reason to use Michael on April 23, in a 12-3 pasting of the Minnesota Twins, but Stick remained on the bench. Ditto four days later, when the Sox rolled to a 9-2 victory over the White Sox. Stick sat.

On May 4, 1976, Red Sox general manager Dick O'Connell called Michael into his office.

"I'm sorry, Stick, we're going to have to let you go," said O'Connell.

Michael, who knew this was coming, had his response planned. Smiling at O'Connell, he said, "Can you tell me what I did wrong?"

The rhetorical nature of the question was not lost on O'Connell. As Michael had never played an inning during his brief tenure with the Red Sox, how could he have failed to do his job?

He was credited with a month or so of big-league service time, which counts toward his pension, but you won't find any mention of the Red Sox if you look Michael up in the *Baseball Encyclopedia*.

But deep inside, Michael knows precisely what he had done wrong. He had played for the Yankees.

"I had heard that there were a couple of guys who were complaining that I shouldn't be with the team," he said. "There was some talk about why they went out and got this guy from the Yankees."

Dozens of ex-Yankees have played for the Red Sox over the years, just as dozens of ex-Red Sox have played for the Yankees. Babe Ruth, anyone? But while Michael was never a star for the Yankees, he had played a significant role in a 1973 brawl between the two teams that fueled the never-to-be-resolved grudge between Red Sox catcher Carlton Fisk and Yankees catcher Thurman Munson.

In the top of the ninth inning of an August 1, 1973 Fenway Park showdown between the Red Sox and Yankees, and with Munson on third base, Michael tried to drop a bunt on a squeeze play. He missed. And now Munson was charging into Fisk, with the resulting collision culminating in a bench-clearing brawl that was of such magnitude that baseball historian Glenn Stout, looking back on the episode years later, wrote: "The rivalry between the two teams that had been dormant for more than 20 years started smoldering again."

Though the Munson-Fisk main bout gets all the attention, let the record show that Michael was heavily involved, throwing wild punches in the pile. Yet, while Fisk and Munson were both ejected, Michael miraculously remained in the game.

Born in Kent, Ohio, on June 2, 1938, Gene Michael played baseball at his local school, Kent State University, before signing with the Pittsburgh Pirates in 1959. He appeared in 30 games with the Pirates in 1966, and then put in a year with the Dodgers before being sold to the Yankees. And it was with the Yankees that Michael found a home, more or less becoming an everyday player, mostly at shortstop, for the next six years. His playing time became more select in 1974 when Jim Mason was acquired from the Texas Rangers.

Michael went on to manage the Yankees for parts of two seasons, and managed the Chicago Cubs in 1986 and 1987. He also had a stint as general manager of the Yankees.

Since then, his duties as one of the Yankees' top troubleshooters have earned him a reputation as one of the game's best talent evaluators and brought him to ballparks throughout North America.

He is a regular visitor to Fenway Park and always enjoys the experience.

"I've always maintained that the rivalry means more to the people up in Boston," Michael said. "But it's there on both sides. It's real. And it's hotter than ever."

In an amusing footnote to this story, in 2002 the Red Sox asked the Yankees for permission to speak with Michael when they were searching for a new general manager.

The Yankees refused. Michael never got a chance to play for the Red Sox, and then he didn't get a chance to run the team that wouldn't let him play.

Where Have You Gone?

JOHN VALENTIN

To John Valentin, it seemed like he'd been fouling off pitches for hours. But now came a fastball from Ricardo Rincon that caught too much of the fat part of the plate, and this time Valentin rifled that pitch to left field left for a double, scoring two runs to give the struggling Red Sox a 5-3 lead over the Cleveland Indians.

The Red Sox needed that hit: Down 0-2 in their best-of-five Division Series against the Indians, they were three innings away from being swept. And Valentin, too, needed that hit: It was his throwing error in the top of the seventh that allowed Kenny Lofton to come across with the tying run for the Indians. And now the packed Fenway house was restless.

"But when I got that hit," said Valentin, "I stood on second base and clapped my hands and said to myself, 'There. I did it.' I always remember that inning because it's what my whole career was all about—don't let stuff get you down. If you make a mistake, just forget about it and come back."

The Red Sox came back mightily against the Indians. They would go on to a 9-3 victory in that October 9, 1999 playoff game, and then win the next two games to capture the series. The Red Sox went on to play the Yankees in the ALCS, losing in five games.

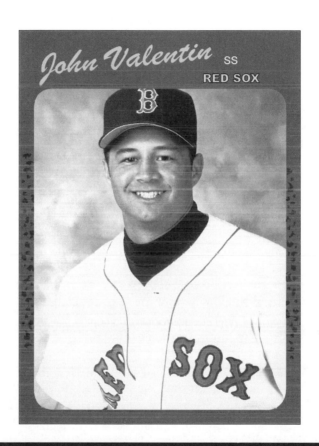

JOHN VALENTIN
Years with Red Sox: 1992-2001

Best Season with Red Sox: 1995 (ninth in MVP Voting)

• Games: 135 • Batting Average: .298 • At Bats: 520 • Hits: 155 •
• Runs: 108 • Home Runs: 27 • RBIs: 102 • Slugging Percentage: .533 •

Valentin still smiles when he thinks about his hit off Rincon. And it still bothers him that the Sox played so poorly against the Yankees.

"No matter what anybody will tell you, everyone who's ever played for the Red Sox wanted to be on the team that finally won the World Series," he said. "And I thought we had a great chance that year, especially when we came back against the Indians. I thought we would beat the Yankees.

"Well, it took another five years, and by that time I was gone, but the Sox finally did it," he said. "And you know what? When they beat the Cardinals in the (2004) World Series, I was thrilled. Except for the end of my career, the Red Sox were the only organization I'd ever played for.

"But I was jealous that they won. I'm not afraid to say that. I wanted to be on the team that won the World Series. That was the dream."

By the summer of 2004, when the Red Sox were getting ready for their playoff run, Valentin was getting ready for a life after baseball—that is, a life after *playing*. Having missed the entire 2003 season, and then, after being cut by the Houston Astros in the last days of spring training, Valentin was mulling a Triple-A offer from the Philadelphia Phillies.

"The Astros cut me because they didn't think I'd stay healthy," Valentin said. "And the Phillies told me they couldn't be sure if they'd call me up. I was going to be insurance. I thought about it, and I realized it was OK to move on and do some other things. I was comfortable with starting a new life."

John and Marie Valentin continued to live in New Jersey with their two children, Justin, born in 1995, and Kendall, born in 1996. But Valentin began making regular commutes to Boston—not to play baseball, but to talk about baseball. He landed a semi-regular gig making appearances on FoxSports New England's *New England Sports Tonight*, as well as with WBZ, Boston's CBS affiliate.

He was interested in television, he said, ". . . because I was willing to say what was on my mind. I was hoping to bring a candid player's perspective to what I was doing."

But while pursuing television, he was also pursuing coaching or managing opportunities. He sent out resumes to people he knew in the game. About a month after the Red Sox won the World Series, he was contacted by the Toronto Blue Jays, who offered him a job as a coach with their Double-A club in Manchester, New Hampshire, about an hour north of Boston.

"I turned down the Phillies because I didn't want to go back to the minors, and then I took a job with the Blue Jays to go back to the minors," said Valentin a few weeks before heading to spring training with his new team. "But this is different. It's one thing to be a player trying to hang on, but, being a coach, it's all new. You can learn the game from a different perspective. You can be a teacher. I haven't ruled out managing in the big leagues, so I'm not afraid of making those bus rides.

"Besides," he said, "I have a lot of unfinished books from my days in the big leagues. This is my chance to get caught up with them."

John Valentin was born on February 18, 1967, in Mineola, New York. He played college baseball at Seton Hall University, and in 1988 he was selected in the fifth round of the June amateur draft. One year later, Valentin's Seton Hall teammate, Mo Vaughn, would also be drafted by the Red Sox.

Valentin hit just .217 in 60 games in his first professional season. Within four years, he was playing shortstop for the Red Sox.

Though a litany of crippling injuries would shorten his career, Valentin still managed 11 seasons in the big leagues. In 1995, he hit .298 with 27 home runs and 102 RBI. And he was a solid postseason performer, hitting .347 with five home runs. He had 12 RBI in the Sox' five games against the Indians in their 1999 Division Series showdown.

"I don't know if I overachieved," said Valentin, "but I don't think, early on, there were too many people who thought I'd play 10 years with the Red Sox. I'll always be proud that I kept fighting and never gave up.

"What I want now," he said, "is to somehow teach that to young players."

Where Have You Gone?

JIM CORSI

For Bernardo Corsi, it was one of those great American success stories. When he moved to the United States from Italy in the early 20th century, he brought with him a talent to build things—especially houses, which provided a nice living when he settled in the Boston area and raised a family.

It was only natural that he wanted his son, Ben, to build houses. Understand that Bernardo Corsi's son fashioned himself something of an athlete, that he especially liked baseball, that he hoped one day to . . . to . . . but, well, there wasn't enough time for baseball. Work came first.

So Ben Corsi, as his father did, built houses. Later, he branched out into commercial construction. But when it came time to raise a family, he vowed that his own kids would have plenty of time for sports—especially baseball.

"Each year, when the Red Sox went to spring training, that was his signal to take us down the cellar so we could hit baseballs against the wall," said his son, Jim Corsi. "I think that's why we did so well in Little League. By the time Little League started, we had already been hitting baseballs for a couple of months."

Turns out Jim Corsi could also *throw* a baseball. His talents took him first to St. Leo's College in Florida, and later to a professional career,

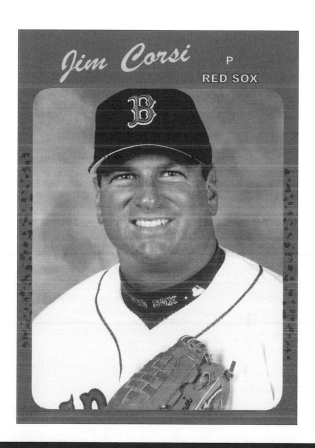

JIM CORSI
Years with Red Sox: 1997-1999

Best Season with Red Sox: 1997

• Games: 52 • Record: 5-3 • ERA: 3.43 • Innings Pitched: 57⅔ •
• Hits Allowed: 56 • Strikeouts: 40 • Walks: 21 • Saves: 2 •

including 10 seasons in the big leagues—three of which were spent with his boyhood team, the Boston Red Sox.

It's a great story. And it leads to an obvious question: What's Jim Corsi doing these days?

Well, let's put it this way: His grandfather, Bernardo Corsi, would have been proud.

"Yeah, I build houses," said Corsi. "Kind of ironic, don't you think? It's something I've always been interested in. I can literally say it's in my blood. Now I'm not saying I'm out there swinging a sledge hammer. Mostly what I do is write checks. But I do a lot of the clearing and I help out here and there when I can."

Even as a minor-league baseball player, Jim Corsi had his grandfather with him in spirit. One year, as Corsi was heading for spring training, Bernardo Corsi gave the kid his pinky ring, saying, "I don't know how much longer I'm going to be around, so I want you to have this."

When Bernardo Corsi died, Jim Corsi attached the ring to a chain he wore around his neck. The ring was with him, on the mound, throughout his big-league career.

Jim Corsi and his wife, Diane, have three children, Julianne, Mitch and Jenna. The kids are all heavily involved with sports. Yet the spirit of Bernardo Corsi lives on: Mitch Corsi, who turned 12 in August of 2004, has a thing about building houses.

"Don't get me wrong—he loves baseball," said Corsi. "But he's always talking about houses. We'll be driving around, and he'll point to different houses and tell me what he likes and doesn't like about the way they were built. He's fascinated by dormers. He'll point to a house and say, 'I liked what they did with the placement of that dormer.' He really knows his stuff."

Born in Newton, Massachusetts, on September 9, 1961, James Bernard Corsi was drafted by the Yankees in 1982, but was released in the minor leagues and then signed by the Red Sox.

From there, the story takes a fascinating turn. After pitching for the Sox' Single-A Greensboro club in 1985, Corsi planned to drive to Florida for spring training in 1986, stopping at St. Leo's College for a couple of weeks to work out.

"I was at St. Leo's when my father called to tell me I'd already been released three weeks earlier," Corsi said. "What happened was, we lived in this house that had had a lot of work done on it, and it had two front doors. One of them led to my father's office, and we never used that door. But we had a new mailman, and he was leaving the mail at the other door. My father finally noticed all the mail, and that's when he found the letter from the Red Sox."

By then, Corsi was already in Florida.

"So I got in my car and drove to Winter Haven," Corsi said. "I said, 'Look, I'm already here. I didn't get your letter. Just let me work out with the team. I promise I'll work harder than anyone here.' And they let me stay."

He began the spring working out with the Single-A pitchers. He ended it as a member of the Sox' Double-A New Britain club, for which he went 2-3 with a 2.28 ERA in 29 relief appearances.

And then the Red Sox released him again.

"They said I proved I could pitch at Double-A, but they didn't think I could pitch at Triple-A," he said. "So I signed with the A's, and a year after that I was in the big leagues. Go figure."

It took a long time, along with stops with the A's, Florida Marlins and Houston Astros, but Corsi finally returned to his hometown team when the Red Sox signed him in 1997. He had one of his best seasons

Photo courtesy of Jim Corsi

in '97, going 5-3 with a 3.43 ERA in 52 relief appearances. The next year he was 3-2 with a 2.59 ERA in a career-high 59 relief appearances.

He closed out his big-league career with the Baltimore Orioles in 1999, and then returned to the Boston area. In addition to building and renovating houses, he has also worked in radio and television. He was a regular on the pre- and post-game shows on the Red Sox-owned NESN for a couple of years.

"But mostly I work on my own, with houses," he said. "I did OK in baseball, but I didn't make enough money not to have to work the rest of my life. I could set it up so I buy a bunch of two-family houses and then live off the rents, but I wouldn't want to be sitting around. I want to work."

And, yes, Jim Corsi still wears the pinky ring on a chain around his neck.

Where Have You Gone?

RUSS GIBSON

It took Russ Gibson 10 years to make it to the big leagues. But when it came time to mapping out his career after baseball, all it took was a simple thank-you note to get things going.

The 10 years in the minors, that's something with which most Red Sox fans are familiar. Born and raised in Fall River, Massachusetts, where he was a baseball and basketball star at Durfee High School, Gibson provided a feel-good angle to the early weeks of the Sox' 1967 "Impossible Dream" season when, after 10 seasons of tank towns, bus rides and cow-milking contests, he finally made the big leagues.

But what few people know about—until now—is the thank-you note that launched Gibson's post-baseball career. Let's have Gibson, who turned 74 during the 2004 season, take it from here.

"This was after I played for the Red Sox," he said. "I played a few seasons with the Giants, and every year during the All-Star break, they had this golf tournament at Lake Tahoe. They'd invite players from the Giants and A's.

"It was a great time. Everything was first class, and everything was free. All you had to do was show up. It was all fantastic—the golf, the food, everything. We had quite a crowd there, too. Dick Dietz. Bobby Bonds. Juan Marichal. Jim Perry.

RUSS GIBSON
Years with Red Sox: 1967-1969

Best Season with Red Sox: 1969

• Games: 85 • Batting Average: .251 • At Bats: 287 • Hits: 72 •
• Runs: 21 • Home Runs: 3 • RBIs: 27 • Slugging Percentage: .321 •

"Well, I got back to San Francisco and I sent a thank-you note to the guy who ran the thing. I didn't think anything of it at the time. I just looked at it as common courtesy."

The man to whom Gibson sent the note was Joe Kowalchuk, whose job was to set up the golf outing. A few weeks later, Kowalchuk got in touch with Gibson, whose career was coming to an end, and asked him what he had planned for himself after baseball. When Gibson replied that he didn't have anything lined up yet, Kowalchuk set him up with a friend from Bank of America, and soon Gibson, stepping down from baseball, was working in the San Francisco offices of Bank of America, in its credit card division.

"When I asked (Kowalchuk) why he was helping me," Gibson said, "he told me, 'In all the time I've been doing this, you're the first person who's written back to me to say thanks.' So I guess it does pay to be courteous."

Gibson worked for Bank of America until 1980, when he returned to his Fall River roots and took a job with the Massachusetts Lottery Commission.

"It was pretty much the same as Bank of America, only instead of helping to sell credit cards I was helping to sell lottery tickets," he said. "Except for this one day, when I actually tried to convince a guy not to buy lottery tickets. I'd go into this small store in Fall River, and there was this guy, this guy I'd known for years, and he'd go in there and buy 30 or 40 tickets at a clip. It looked like he was just blowing all his money, so I said to him, 'I don't think you should be buying so many of those things.' And he just told me to mind my own business."

Gibson's early claim to fame with the '67 Red Sox is that he was behind the plate when rookie lefthander Billy Rohr, making his first major-league start, pitched a one-hitter against the Yankees at Yankee Stadium. The no-hit bid ended with a ninth-inning single to right by Elston Howard, who would play for the Red Sox later in the season.

"So many people talk about that being Rohr's first game, but what's crazy about it is that it was also my first game," said Gibson. "I went out to the mound at one point to quiet him down, and as I was saying the words I was thinking to myself, 'What the hell am I talking about? This is my first game and I'm as nervous as he is.'"

Gibson thought he had made the big-league roster as early as 1964, and was even told by a clubhouse attendant late in spring training that he was a lock to be with the club on Opening Day. An hour later, he was called into manager Johnny Pesky's office and sent back to the minors.

"I was going to quit and find something else to do with my life," he said. "But a year later Dick Williams was hired to be manager of our Triple-A club in Toronto, and he asked me to be his player-coach. And when they ask you to be a player-coach in the minors, you pretty much know you're not going to the big leagues."

When Williams was named manager of the Red Sox for the 1967 season, he made it known he had a job for Gibson. A job? Gibson thought he was going to be a coach. Instead, Williams gave him a chance to make the team as a player. On April 14, 1967, when an excited Billy Rohr walked out to the Yankee Stadium mound to throw his first big-league pitch, his catcher was an equally excited Russ Gibson.

Gibson went on to play three seasons with the Red Sox, and three more with the Giants. He retired from the Lottery Commission in October, 2003, and he and his wife, Ann, live quietly in the Fall River area. He was offered a scouting job by the Toronto Blue Jays, he said, but turned it down because he wasn't keen on the travel that would have been involved. He has two sons, Chris, a police officer in nearby Somerset, and Greg, a former Air Force pilot who now works for General Electric.

Russ Gibson still makes the occasional trip to Fenway Park, where aging Sox fans corner him and ask him about the fabled '67 season. If you ever run into Gibby, feel free to ask the man for his autograph.

But don't forget to say thank you. You never know what it could lead to.

BILLY HARRELL

Billy Harrell didn't know it at the time, but he spent the last few years of his professional baseball career preparing for his life *after* baseball.

One of the first African-Americans to play for the Red Sox, Harrell appeared in 37 games as a utility infielder in 1961, hitting just .162. But the Sox liked Harrell enough to keep him in their farm system for the next three seasons, first at Seattle, then Toronto, and he became a minor league player/coach with the Sox in 1966, possibly the first black man to coach at any level for the club.

"I spent a lot of time working with the younger players when they sent me to the minors," Harrell said. "I was a player, but, in a way, I was also a coach even before they actually made me a coach. We might have a younger player who was homesick, or not ready to play pro ball. Well, I'd spend a lot of time counseling that player."

Is it any wonder, then, that when Harrell's career ended he worked for the state of New York as a youth counselor?

Working with kids was something Harrell had hoped to do earlier in his life, when he was studying at Siena College. But he had been a two-sport star at Sienna—basketball and baseball—and when his college days ended he received offers to play professionally.

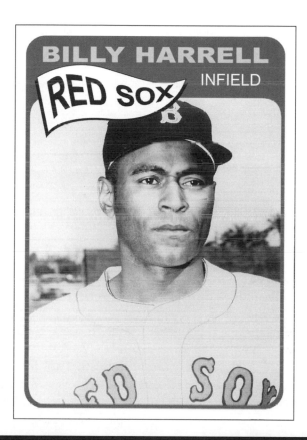

BILLY HARRELL
Year with Red Sox: 1961

Best Season with Red Sox: 1961

• Games: 37 • Batting Average: .162 • At Bats: 37 • Hits: 6 •
• Runs: 10 • Home Runs: 0 • RBIs: 1 • Stolen Bases: 1 •

The barnstorming Harlem Globetrotters wanted to sign him. So, too, did the old Minneapolis Lakers of the National Basketball Association. Instead, he chose the path that led to baseball, signing with the Cleveland Indians in 1952.

Why baseball?

"Money was tight in those days, as you can imagine," said Harrell, who turned 76 during the 2004 season. "The Indians offered me $15,000, so, you bet, I played baseball."

He returned home to Troy, New York, with his wife, Vivian, when his baseball career ended. His college training and his interests led him to youth counseling, and he spent most of the next three decades working with at-risk teens.

"Sometimes, it was just getting up a softball game and getting the kids outdoors," he said. "Sometimes, it meant going into the parents' house and trying to figure out what was going wrong. And that was when you had parents yelling at you, asking what you were doing here, saying, 'Who do you think you are telling us how to raise are kids?' Things like that.

"And we had a lot of success stories," he said. "I don't think any of them grew up to be governor, but a lot of them grew up to get jobs, own homes, raise kids of their own. I hear from some of them from time to time. It makes you feel a little good inside to know you might have played a role in making them better people. It was the work I always thought I'd be doing."

William "Billy" Harrell was born on July 18, 1928 in Norristown, Pennsylvania. His family later relocated to Troy, New York, when his father, John Nurney Harrell, found a better-paying job at a Coke plant. It was in Troy that young Billy learned to play both baseball and basketball, which led to Siena College.

Before signing with the Indians, he had a brief stint with the Saratoga Harlem Yankees of the American Basketball League, which included an exhibition game against the Boston Celtics. His ABL days behind him, and having turned down the Globetrotters—he still has the telegram inviting him to join—Harrell plunged into his baseball career, hoping to make the big leagues. In 1953, playing for the Reading Indians, a Cleveland farm team, Harrell and future big-league star Rocky Colavito helped lead their team to a 101-47 record. Colavito led the Eastern League in home runs and RBI, and Harrell hit .330. Both players were inducted into the Reading Baseball Hall of Fame in 2001.

On September 2, 1955, Harrell made his major-league debut with the Cleveland Indians. He would play parts of three seasons with the Indians as a utility infielder, but there were also many days and nights back in the minor leagues, and he figured his big-league days were over, when, after being picked up by the St. Louis Cardinals, he spent all of 1959 and '60 on the farm.

Then came a surprise: The Red Sox claimed Harrell in the Rule V Draft, and in spring training, 1961, he made the club as a utility infielder.

Despite his lack of playing time, the season wasn't without its memories—not just for Billy Harrell, but for his son, Bill.

"They had one of those father-son games, and it was right around the time I was going into Little League," said Bill Harrell, a retired Air Force sergeant. "I thought we were going to play in an actual game. So I get there, and they have the bases all moved in and we're playing with a tennis ball. I remember swinging at the ball and running to first base, and then turning to my father and saying, 'Is this it?' I call my father every day, and that's one of the things we still joke about."

Bill Harrell still has the pint-sized Red Sox uniform he wore in that game, the boy's only day in the big leagues. As for the old man, his big-league career ended with that '61 season. He played the next three seasons in Seattle and Toronto, and in 1965 he joined the Sox' Pittsfield club. He also did some scouting for the Red Sox before settling in Troy and becoming a youth counselor and, later, a probation officer.

Harrell has five children. In addition to Bill, he has three daughters, Tanya, Christine and Diane. He has eight grandchildren. Harrell's first marriage ended in divorce. He and his second wife, Miriam, live in Albany, New York.

BILL MONBOUQUETTE

Bill Monbouquette had a schoolboy crush. The girl's name was Josephine Ritchie. She had long, beautiful hair and a fantastic smile, and she lived just a couple of doors down from the Monbouquette place, on Elliott Street in Medford, Massachusetts.

Josephine loved to dance. What she didn't much like was baseball, and it so happened that Bill Monbouquette was the star pitcher for the varsity at Medford High School. And so it was that when Bill politely asked that pretty girl from 24 Elliot Street out on a date, Josephine Ritchie very politely replied that she wasn't interested.

Nothing personal, she said. It's just that she didn't want to date a baseball player.

This was in 1955. Now let's fast forward four decades, to the 40th reunion of the Medford High School Class of '55. Monbouquette had indeed been a baseball player—he pitched 11 seasons in the big leagues, along with spending many, many years as a minor-league pitching coach—but by now he viewed himself as just another kid from the Class of '55, looking to pal around with some of the kids from the old days.

The first guy he ran into was his old baseball teammate, Charlie Pagliarulo. Now Pags never went on to the big leagues, but his son,

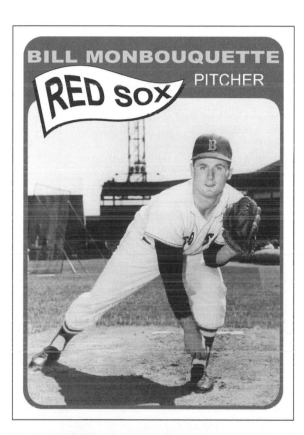

BILL MONBOUQUETTE
Years with Red Sox: 1958-1965

Best Season with Red Sox: 1963 (All Star)

• Games: 37 • Record: 20-10 • ERA: 3.81 • Innings Pitched: 266⅔ •
• Hits Allowed: 158 • Strikeouts: 174 • Walks: 42 • Complete Games: 13 •

Mike, became a star with the New York Yankees and later played on a World Series winner with the Minnesota Twins.

. So the two old teammates talked for a while—talked a little baseball, talked about the old days—and then Bill Monbouquette mentioned his schoolboy crush on Josephine Ritchie.

"Well, you're in luck," said Pagliarulo. "She's standing right over there."

Monbouquette, 59 at the time, and divorced, summoned up the courage—again—to ask Josephine out on a date.

And they've been together ever since.

"It's not that I didn't like him when we were in high school," said Josephine, who never married until she and Bill, after being together for eight years, finally tied the knot in November of 2003. "I liked him a lot. But I didn't like him *romantically*. To him, it was all about sports in those days. All I thought about were things like dances and the prom."

The Bill Monbouquette from the Medford High days was a good enough pitcher to be courted by the Red Sox, Tigers and Cubs. He finally settled on the Red Sox, not so much for the money—he received a $4,000 bonus—but because, all things being equal, he wanted to pitch for his hometown team.

He made his major-league debut on July 18, 1958 and went on to become one of the team's finest pitchers in the early '60s. He pitched a no-hitter against the White Sox on August 1, 1962, and in 1963, pitching for a team that would finish in seventh place, Monbouquette had a career year, going 20-10. He was a career 114-112 pitcher.

Monbouquette also played a significant role in the social history of the Red Sox. In 1959, during a game against the Chicago White Sox, an aging Red Sox coach named Del Baker began hurling racial epithets at the White Sox' Minnie Minoso, who was from Cuba. Standing nearby was Pumpsie Green, who had recently become the first African-American to play for the Red Sox.

It was Monbouquette, confirmed Green, who walked over to the 68-year-old Baker and told him, in no uncertain terms, to knock it off.

To understand why Monbouquette defended Green, some background is in order. Monbouquette grew up in West Medford, an important stop on the legendary "Underground Railroad" that helped spirit escaped slaves to Canada before the Civil War. Following the Civil War, the neighborhood was settled by freed slaves, and continued to be heavily populated by African-Americans at the time Monbouquette was growing up.

"Black kids would hang around with white kids, and vice-versa," said Monbouquette. "It just wasn't a big deal. We went to the same schools. We played sports together. As for what happened that day with Del Baker, I looked over at Pumpsie and could see he was upset by what was happening. He was a good kid. He didn't deserve to have people talking in front of him like that."

Monbouquette's playing career ended when he was released by the San Francisco Giants at the end of spring training in 1969. He considered going back to the minors, but, at 32 years old, he wasn't keen on riding the buses again.

Which is all kind of funny, considering that Monbouquette has spent most of the last 30-plus years as a scout and minor-league pitching coach. He has coached in the minors for the Yankees, Mets, Blue Jays and Tigers, and for a spell was big-league pitching coach for the Mets and Blue Jays. In recent years he has served as pitching coach for the Tigers' Oneonta club in the short-season New York Penn League.

"I like working with the kids," he said. "You like to think you can have an impact on their lives, their careers. It's a good feeling when you connect with them."

One of those kids was Mike Timlin, who had Monbouquette as a coach when he was a Toronto Blue Jays minor-leaguer.

"I met Monbo when I was playing for Myrtle Beach in 1988," said Timlin. "I didn't have that killer instinct back then, and he continuously hounded me on that. He said to me one day, "Those hitters, they're trying to take something away from you. You've got to prevent that from happening.'

"And," said Timlin, "he taught me the sinker I'm still throwing today. He took me aside one day, and said, 'Just grip the ball like this and throw it.' Well, I threw it, and it sunk so much that I couldn't get it to the plate. I finally perfected it, and that's his pitch I'm using when I'm out there."

Along with the hundreds of baseball kids Monbouquette has coached over the years, he has three real kids—Marc, a pilot for American Airlines; Michel, a Marine colonel; and Merric, a New Hampshire-based professional log-roller.

Monbouquette was inducted into the Red Sox Hall of Fame in 2000.

Where Have You Gone?

RICH GEDMAN

Minor-league baseball teams are really dream factories, filled with hopeful kids who view every at-bat, every pitch, every catch, as a step toward making it to the big time.

Yet when Rich Gedman arrived at Triple-A Columbus in 1993, he had left his dreams back home in Massachusetts. Oh, he was absolutely hoping he'd be promoted by the parent New York Yankees if the need arose, but that's not what this minor-league assignment was all about.

Now, he was just looking to have a little fun.

After more than a decade with the Red Sox, he had been recast as a journeyman backup catcher, playing a little with the Houston Astros and then putting in a couple of seasons with the St. Louis Cardinals. A few months prior to accepting a minor-league assignment with the Yankees, he had been released in spring training by the Oakland A's.

"To be honest, I was worn down," he said. "I always loved the game, and I always will, but you talk to any player and he'll tell you there are times when it gets to you—the politics, the expectations, the travel. I was done."

He paused, and then said, "But I asked myself, 'Is it me, or is it the game?' That's when I decided to go to Columbus. I decided I was going to play there for the rest of the season, just for the joy of the game, and bring some finality to my career. And you know what? That season in Columbus may have been the most fun I ever had.

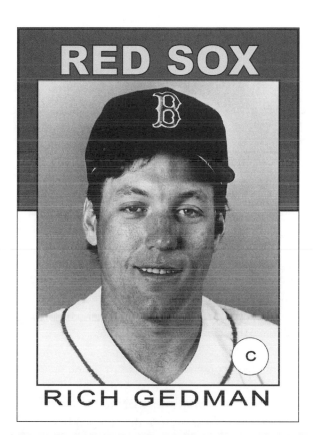

RED SOX

RICH GEDMAN

RICH GEDMAN
Years with Red Sox: 1980-1990

Best Season with Red Sox: 1985 (All Star)

• Games: 144 • Batting Average: .295 • At Bats: 498 • Hits: 147 •
• Runs: 66 • Home Runs: 18 • RBIs: 80 • Slugging Percentage: .484 •

"The thing is, there was a moment there I thought the Yankees were going to call me up. Matt Nokes got hurt. But they already had Mike Stanley and Jim Leyritz up there, so they decided to go with an outfielder. They brought up Gerald Williams. Yes, I wish they had called me up. But I kept having fun, and that's how I finished the season. And I've been comfortable with baseball ever since."

During his days with the Red Sox, Gedman was special in that he was *local*. Like Tony Conigliaro and Harry Agganis and Jerry Remy and so many others before him, Gedman was a Massachusetts native, raised a Red Sox fan. Gedman was born on September 26, 1959 in Worcester, which means that as an eight-year-old he got to root for the Sox in the 1967 World Series.

Just 13 years later, on September 7, 1980, Gedman made his major-league debut with the Red Sox. He was a couple of weeks shy of his 21st birthday.

Though he would spend some time back in the minors in 1981, he was soon back with the Red Sox, who, having lost future Hall of Famer Carlton Fisk to the Chicago White Sox, planted him behind the plate and hoped he'd mature into the job.

He did. Appearing in 81 games in 1983, Gedman hit .294. In 1984, he hit 24 home runs. In 1985, he had perhaps his best all-around season, hitting .295 with 18 home runs and 80 RBI. He was an all-star in both '85 and '86.

And, yes, he was Boston's catcher in the 1986 World Series against the Mets, meaning he was behind the plate in Game 6, the Red Sox just one pitch away from winning their first Series since 1918. Trailing 5-3 in the bottom of the 10th inning, the Mets rallied for three runs to win the game when Mookie Wilson's grounder skipped horribly (in the eyes of Red Sox fans) between the legs of first baseman Bill Buckner. The inning also included a wild pitch by Red Sox reliever Bob Stanley, a scorer's call that some believe should have been a passed ball on Gedman.

Though he didn't know it at the time, Gedman's best seasons were already behind him. He was a late arrival to the team in 1987 after having declared free-agency, and what followed was a series of medical setbacks—a groin injury, followed by torn ligaments in his left thumb. He appeared in just 52 games. He hit .205.

Whether it was injuries, or his faithful adherence to the teaching of Red Sox batting guru Walt Hriniak, or the pressure that comes when you're a hometown fan being booed by the hometown fans, Gedman was never able to dust himself off and become an all-star again.

By 1989, he was platooning with veteran catcher Rick Cerone, with Cerone usually starting against lefthanders and Gedman, a left-handed hitter, facing right-handers. One night at Chicago's Comiskey Park, Red Sox manager Joe Morgan puzzled the beat writers covering the team when he started Cerone against the White Sox' Shawn Hillegas—a righthander. Facing Hillegas in the sixth inning, Cerone snapped a 3-3 tie with a two-run homer and the Red Sox went on to an 8-4 victory.

Everyone had assumed this was yet another example of "Morgan Magic," with the crusty native of Walpole, Massachusetts, defying baseball logic and being proved right. Yet when he met with reporters, Morgan admitted that he had confused Shawn *Hillegas* with Paul *Kilgus*, a lefthander who was pitching for the cross-town Chicago Cubs.

"But when I figured it out, I said, 'What the hell,'" said Morgan.

Everyone laughed. Gedman probably didn't find it so funny.

Yet when his career was over, he had spent 13 seasons in the big leagues, with a .252 average, not bad for a catcher. He had been an All-Star. Twice. He played in the World Series, collecting three hits in Game 4 and hitting a home run in Game 7. He hit .357 in two American League Championship Series.

"And I think that's what helped me when I was in Columbus in '93— I had accomplished things," he said. "Now, I could look at those kids and see in their eyes that they wanted to do some of the things I had done.

"They had that hope, that desire. And it was natural. It wasn't all hype or invention. They were knocking on the door. I know it sounds corny, but I was at peace with baseball."

Though he took a shot at making the Baltimore Orioles in 1994, he refused yet another assignment to the minors, explaining, "I didn't want to turn into Crash Davis," referring to Kevin Costner's character in the movie *Bull Durham*.

He returned home to Massachusetts and to his wife, Sherry, and their three kids: Michael, born in 1987; Matt, born in 1988; and Marissa, born in 1992.

He has remained in baseball as the assistant coach at the Belmont Hill School, a private school outside Boston. In 2005 he began his third season as a coach with the North Shore Spirit of the independent Northeast League, teaming up with manager John Kennedy and pitching coach Dick Radatz, both former Red Sox players.

Where Have You Gone?

DOMINIC
DiMAGGIO

Though often overshadowed by his older brother's Hall of Fame talents and global celebrity, Dominic DiMaggio was a solid big-leaguer in his own right, a career .298 hitter whose speed and reach in center field made him one of the top defensive players of his time.

Yet it's possible that the bespectacled Little Professor, as he was known, saved his greatest Fenway Park moment for much later in his life—after his older brother Joe had passed away, and, most important for this discussion, a few days following the death of the greatest Red Sox player of all time, Ted Williams.

The heartbreaking saga of Williams's so-called golden years has been well-chronicled. He was, in the opinion of many, reduced to little more than a human souvenir factory by his son, John-Henry Williams, and the story grew still sadder, morbidly so, in the days following Teddy Ballgame's death. It was then that John-Henry arranged to have his father's remains delivered to an Arizona-based cryogenics facility for freezing and storage, the idea being that "the greatest hitter who ever lived" would be gloriously resurrected in the far-off future, once the necessary medical advances were in place to make it all possible.

Friends of Ted Williams insisted the old ballplayer had wished to have his remains cremated, his ashes scattered near a favored fishing

DOM DiMAGGIO
OUTFIELD

DOM DiMAGGIO
Years with Red Sox: 1940-1953

Best Season with Red Sox: 1950 (All Star, sixth in MVP voting)

• Games: 141 • Batting Average: .328 • At Bats: 588 • Hits: 193 •
• Runs: 131 • Home Runs: 7 • RBIs: 70 • Stolen Bases: 15 •

place off the Florida coast. Included among those friends was Dom DiMaggio.

On July 22, 2002, the Red Sox opened up Fenway Park for an elaborate, tasteful celebration of Williams's life. More than 20,000 fans solemnly filed into Fenway for the occasion, and dozens of former Red Sox players, in period uniform, were in attendance. Even Jack Fisher, the man who in 1960 served up the pitch that Williams hit for a dramatic home run in his last at-bat, stood on the Fenway Park mound in his old Baltimore Orioles uniform as broadcaster Curt Gowdy re-enacted his call of the historic smash.

Many wondered if the swirling debate over the handling of Williams's remains would be mentioned on this night that was, after all, advertised as the celebration of a great life.

And nothing was said . . . until Dom DiMaggio, 85 years old at the time, delivered an impassioned plea on behalf of his longtime friend and teammate.

"I am saddened by the turmoil of the current controversy," he said. "I hope and pray this controversy will end as abruptly as it began, and the family will do the right thing by honoring (Ted's) final resting place, and may he rest in peace."

Fenway Park erupted with applause. For DiMaggio had uttered the words that were on the minds of virtually everyone in attendance, words that needed to be heard. And while it was one thing for preachy sports columnists and fire-breathing talk-show hosts to stand up for Ted Williams, it was a riveting, never-to-be-forgotten moment when one of No. 9's closest friends made known his sentiments.

"When I was invited to attend the event, I called the Red Sox and spoke with (executive vice president of public affairs) Charles Steinberg," said DiMaggio. "I told him I'd be pleased to come, but that there were a few words I'd like to say.

"I was stunned by what was happening to Ted after he died," said DiMaggio. "I didn't know if anything I said would help change things, but I had to speak my mind."

Despite DiMaggio's plea, John-Henry Williams continued with his cryogenics plan, insisting he was acting upon his father's wishes. John-Henry would himself die two years later, reportedly of leukemia.

Though the events following Williams's death nudged DiMaggio back into the sports spotlight for the first time in decades, he had never been too far away from Fenway Park. He became a hugely successful entrepreneur in the Boston area following the end of his playing career, investing in a variety of businesses.

He supplied carpeting for automobiles and material for roof insulation. He manufactured rubberized material for upholstery and bedding, as well as material used for packaging.

Though he failed in his bid to purchase the Red Sox following the death of Thomas A. Yawkey, DiMaggio had already made his entrée into sports team ownership as one of the original investors in the Boston Patriots of the American Football League. The team's principal owner was Billy Sullivan, who had once been publicity director of the old Boston Braves—at the same time DiMaggio was playing center field for the Red Sox. When the Patriots needed a facility to play their home games, it was DiMaggio, the businessman who could get things done, who approached the Red Sox about securing Fenway Park.

Born in San Francisco on February 12, 1917, Dominic DiMaggio followed in the footsteps of his brothers, Joe, who became a Yankee for life in 1936, and Vince, a well-traveled outfielder who made his major-league debut with the Boston Braves in 1937. Dominic DiMaggio's road to the big leagues also took him to Boston, but to the Red Sox, for whom he debuted on April 16, 1940. His best season was 1950, when he hit .328. Dominic and Emily DiMaggio live comfortably in Marion, Massachusetts, but they also have a home in Florida and continue to make occasional trips to San Francisco, where they have investment properties.

Though DiMaggio is quick to say, "I'm getting old and cranky," his former Red Sox teammate Johnny Pesky has a more concise take on things: "Ever since he had that bypass surgery, he thinks he's a kid again. He probably wants to come back and play again, and I wouldn't put it past him."

The DiMaggios have two sons, Paul and Peter, and a daughter, Emily. In December, 2004, they closed up their Massachusetts home and flew down to Florida for a couple of weeks, jetted out to San Francisco to take care of some financial business, and then headed south to Phoenix to spend Christmas with their daughter and some of their grandchildren.

Even in his mid-80s, Dom DiMaggio was still covering a lot of ground.

Where Have You Gone?

PUMPSIE GREEN

Through most of the 1950s, the Red Sox were a collection of affable, well-paid white guys, teeming with spring training promise but, inevitably, safely removed from the pennant fight come Labor Day. But when the Red Sox arrived for spring training in Scottsdale, Arizona, in February of '59, the two hot topics in camp were that this might be Ted Williams's final season . . . and that a black man, Elijah Jerry "Pumpsie" Green, had a chance to make the team.

As far back as the 1958 season, Green was already being rumored as a future member of the Red Sox, with the *Boston American* stating that he ". . . will be the first colored player to make the Red Sox roster—and that could happen next spring."

Still, spring training 1959 came and went. And Green was sent back to the minors. As for Williams's departure, that, too, proved premature, with Teddy Ballgame continuing to play with the Sox until the end of the 1960 season.

But in the early-morning hours of July 21, 1959, Green received a telephone call from George Brophy, general manager of the Minneapolis Millers of the Triple-A American Association.

Green was playing for the Millers, a Boston farm club, and playing well. Having entered the season as the "hottest" Red Sox prospect in the

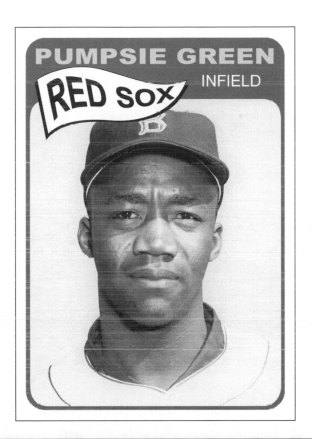

PUMPSIE GREEN
Years with Red Sox: 1959-1962

Best Season with Red Sox: 1961

• Games: 88 • Batting Average: .260 • At Bats: 219 • Hits: 57 •
• Runs: 33 • Home Runs: 6 • RBIs: 27 • Slugging Percentage: .425 •

opinion of *The Sporting News*, Green was now hitting .320 for the Millers.

"Are you up?" asked Brophy.

"Well, I am now," said Green.

"You're going to the big leagues," said Brophy. "The Red Sox are bringing you up."

Later that night, at Chicago's old Comiskey Park, the newly minted Red Sox infielder pinch ran for Vic Wertz in the eighth inning and remained in the game at shortstop.

He was black and in the big leagues and wearing a Red Sox uniform. The Red Sox finally had a black player. (Strange but true: With Willie O'Ree making his National Hockey League debut in 1958, the Boston Bruins had a black player on their roster a year before the Red Sox did.)

Though he did show occasional flashes of brilliance, Pumpsie Green did not enjoy a stellar big-league career. He played parts of four seasons with the Red Sox, and then had a 17-game stint with the Mets in 1963. He was a lifetime .246 hitter.

But because the notoriously behind-the-times Red Sox were the last team to promote an African-American player to the big leagues, and because Pumpsie Green happened to be that player, life would never be the same for the Oakland, California, native.

"For a long time, nobody said anything, nobody called, and I just went on to live my life," said Green, who returned to his Bay Area roots and coached high school baseball for many years. "But then, over the years, more and more people would call. Usually, they just wanted to ask about my being called up by the Red Sox and all that, and I don't mind telling the story.

"But then, whenever there was some racial issue in baseball, or particularly on the Red Sox, people would call me and expect me to provide all the answers. And I admit I got a little tired of that after a while. I don't have all the answers."

Bill Russell, a onetime San Francisco basketball standout who went on to make history with the Boston Celtics, had talked with Green before the 1959 season, advising him who he could trust and which places he should avoid, should he be called up by the Red Sox.

"But nothing ever happened to me in Boston that hadn't already happened someplace else," said Green. "And . . . the Red Sox were always good to me. I remember only one incident. They had this old coach, his name was Del Baker, and he was saying some things one night, using some words. He wasn't even talking to me. It was a game against the Cleveland Indians. This was when they had Minnie Minoso, who was born in Cuba. Del was using these words—I don't ever want to repeat them, they were derogatory words—and he knew I was there. I just looked at him, wondering what I should do, and (pitcher) Bill Monbouquette just got up, walked over to him, and said, 'Del, Pumpsie's here now. You can't talk that way anymore.'"

There were, of course, the various incidents around town, along with the subtle racism that existed on the Red Sox even when Green was with the club. Remember, this is the franchise that offered a sham tryout to Negro League stars Jackie Robinson, Sam Jethroe and Marvin Williams in 1945, and then never even got back to the three men. This is the same franchise that could have bought, for a measly $5,000, a young Negro League outfielder named Willie Mays. But passed. And, yes, this is the same franchise that waited 12 years after Robinson's debut with the Brooklyn Dodgers to break their own whites-only policy.

And that's why Pumpsie Green will remain an important figure in Red Sox history even if, at times, the questions become tedious.

"But I do like to just sit back and talk baseball—just baseball," said Green, who turned 71 in October, 2004. "I've become a big San Francisco Giants fan. I love watching Barry Bonds play. He's just incredible."

Green remained in the game via his coaching career at Berkeley High School. He worked for many years as a security officer at the school as well, and was a longtime fixture in the Berkeley Recreation Department.

"I go to the YMCA every day," he said. "I believe in keeping active. I'll always be that way."

Green is kept busy by the many women in his life—his wife, Marie, and a teenaged granddaughter, Brittany, who Pumpsie lovingly drives around town. And Pumpsie dutifully looks after his mother, who turned 90 in 2004.

"I have no worries," said Green. "Well, I have one: I worry that, one of these days, the Red Sox are going to play the Giants in the World Series. If that happens, I'm not going to know who to root for. Well, I'm guessing I'll be leaning toward the Giants—I mean, this is my home out here—but it'll be tough if they're playing the Red Sox."

Where Have You Gone?

DENNIS "OIL CAN" BOYD

D ennis "Oil Can" Boyd picked up the thick, blue uniform and laughed. "I know about this team," he said, examining the fabric. "This is the Ethiopian Clowns. It was an old Negro League barnstorming team. Played all over the place. Played anyone, any time. Those guys must have had some fun, you know?"

And then, seeking to have some fun of his own, the 44-year-old former Red Sox pitcher climbed into the uniform, pounded a fist into his glove and said, "Let's go play baseball."

This was on August 19, 2004, at St. Peter's Field in Cambridge, Massachusetts, just a few miles from Fenway Park. The event was the 2004 Fleet Boston Oldtime Baseball Game, an annual summertime charity game featuring mostly college-aged players decked out in a dizzying array of old-style uniforms. The 2004 game was being played as a benefit for the radiation oncology center at Cambridge's Mount Auburn Hospital, and Boyd and former NFL star Steve DeOssie were the evening's marquee attractions.

As noted in the introduction of this book, I am one of the game's organizers. I had run into Boyd about a month earlier at Fenway Park, where the Can was doing a corporate event, and, as is always the case with this man, the talk was all about baseball.

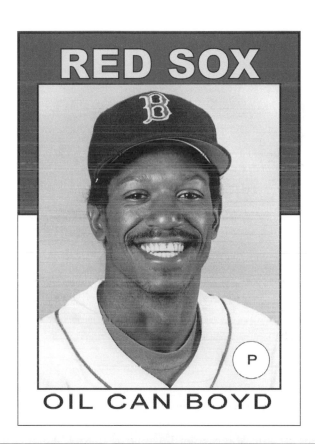

"OIL CAN" BOYD
Years with Red Sox: 1982-1989

Best Season with Red Sox: 1986

• Games: 30 • Record: 16-10 • ERA: 3.78 • Innings Pitched: 214⅓ •
• Hits Allowed: 222 • Strikeouts: 129 • Walks: 45 • Complete Games: 10 •

Standing near third base, he started yakking about Wade Boggs, his former Red Sox teammate.

"Everyone talks about him as a hitter," said Boyd, "but I don't think he gets enough credit as a fielder. I think if you check all my old boxs-cores you'll find that Boggs never made an error in a game I started. He was always there for me."

And then Boyd started talking about the old Negro Leagues, to him a beloved topic of conversation. He was talking about the Homestead Grays, Kansas City Monarchs and other nines from the old Negro League days, and that's when it occurred to me that the Can should be playing in the Oldtime Baseball Game.

"Maybe," I said, "you could come out of retirement and throw a few innings."

After all, I said to Boyd, we usually invite a retired big-leaguer or two to add spice to the game. Former Yankees third baseman Mike Pagliarulo, who grew up in the Boston area, had played in the game four times. Jim Corsi, another Boston area native and former big-league pitcher, had made a couple of appearances.

"Sounds great," said Boyd. "Just give me the date and the time and how to get there, and I'll be there."

And sure enough, Boyd showed up that night, bringing with him his wife, Karen, and their two children, Dennis and Tala.

Never mind pitching a couple of innings. Boyd, who been out of the big leagues since 1991 and hadn't pitched in a game since his independ-ent minor-league career ended in 1997 because of a blood clot in his right shoulder, worked *four* innings that night. And still he didn't want to come out. (He gave up a home run to Harvard University's Zak Farkes, but took solace in the fact that just two months earlier Farkes had been selected by the Red Sox in the June amateur draft.)

Boyd's appearance that night in Cambridge—which, by the way, was a huge hit with the 1,500 or so fans in attendance at the tiny ballpark—simply confirmed what anybody who ever met the Can will quickly tell you: The guy always loved baseball.

True, he wasn't always a manager's delight. Boyd had his own way of doing things, and he also had a temper. There was a nasty scene one year when he wasn't selected to participate in the All-Star Game. After a rough outing in Game 3 of the 1986 World Series, he privately wept when a day of rain enabled Sox manager John McNamara to skip over Boyd for Game 7, choosing, instead, Bruce Hurst.

But for a stringbean of a man, he could surely pitch. Generously listed as 6-1 and tipping the scales at a measly 155 pounds, Boyd had a good fastball and a deceptive delivery. He won 78 games over his 10 years in the big leagues, mostly with the Red Sox. His best season was in 1986, when he posted a 16-10 record and 3.78 ERA, helping the Red Sox to the American League pennant.

But the Red Sox kicked the Can following the 1989 season—they let him declare for free agency, and didn't opt to re-sign him. He wound up with the Montreal Expos, for whom he won 10 games in 1990, and he closed out the '91 season with the Texas Rangers.

And then he returned home to his native Meridian, Mississippi, his career over.

But he was hardly through with baseball. He pitched for several independent minor-league teams in the 90s, and continues to busy himself with baseball camps and clinics, as well as making personal appearances on behalf of the Red Sox, whose new owners have welcomed him back to the organizational family.

Photo courtesy of Dennis Boyd

He looks great. There's some gray cavorting with his otherwise dark hair, but he says he's only put on "three or four pounds since I stopped playing, and if I work up a good sweat I'll get that out of me real quick."

The Can always had a way with words. He is famously remembered for that night in Cleveland, when, after a game at old Cleveland Stadium was fogged out, he said, "That's what they get for building a stadium on the ocean."

He mingles well with fans. Hardly a day goes by without someone asking him how he got his nickname. (In Boyd's neck of the woods, the locals refer to beer as "oil cans," and, well, our man always liked his oil. Hence . . .)

Though he splits his time between Providence, Rhode Island, and Meridian, Mississippi, he hopes one day to bring an independent minor-league team to his boyhood home.

Oil Can Boyd? Running a baseball team?

"You have to love the game and work real hard," he said. "That's me both ways."

Where Have You Gone?

BILLY ROHR

The *Baseball Encyclopedia* is filled with the names of players whose careers came and went without a whole lot of fuss. We're talking not about the stars of the game, but its lesser-known players, guys who may well have had respectable careers but who, in the end, are names lost in history to the generations of fans who followed.

And then there is Billy Rohr. On the day he pitched his first game in the big leagues, he became a never-to-be-forgotten character in Red Sox history, his name so familiar that, even today, many New England baseball fans who weren't even alive at the time understand the importance of what happened at Yankee Stadium on April 14, 1967.

It was the Yankees' home opener. Pitching for the Yankees was one of the great lefthanders of his time, Whitey Ford. Pitching for the Red Sox was lanky 21-year-old lefthander Billy Rohr, who had never thrown so much as a pitch in the big leagues.

Considering that neither the Yankees nor Red Sox were projected as pennant contenders in 1967, this chilly April matchup offered no hints at making history. But that's the funny thing about baseball: Any game, on any day, has the potential to become a photograph of the mind that you'll never, ever forget.

BILLY ROHR
Year with Red Sox: 1967

Best Season with Red Sox: 1967

• Games: 10 • Record: 2-3 • ERA: 5.10 • Innings Pitched: 42⅓ •
• Hits Allowed: 43 • Strikeouts: 16 • Walks: 22 • Complete Games: 2 •

And so it was on this day, as the kid pitcher, making his first appearance in the big leagues, carried a no-hitter into the ninth inning. Tom Tresh led off the bottom of the ninth with a deep smash to left, but Carl Yastrzemski hauled in the ball with one of the greatest catches in Red Sox history.

When Joe Pepitone flied to right, Rohr was one out away from pitching a no-hitter.

Up stepped Elston Howard, who would end the 1967 season catching for the Red Sox in the World Series. But on this day he was a veteran member of the Yankees, and he lofted a pitch from Rohr to right field for a base hit, ending the rookie's no-hit bid.

Nearly 40 years later, sportswriters, fans and history buffs still seek out Billy Rohr to ask him about his magical day at Yankee Stadium.

"Well, it makes it more fun for me," he said. "It was one brief moment in baseball, my 15 minutes of fame. But those 15 minutes are dying hard. Several times a year, people call and ask about the one-hitter. Every time it looks like the Red Sox are going to make a run, I'll receive a bunch of calls. And I get a lot of calls in April, as the anniversary approaches.

"The one thing that bothers me," he said, "is that every time someone writes a story about me, it always ends with Elston Howard getting a hit in the ninth inning. As hard as you (media) guys scratch around for a fresh angle and decorate your writing with events that may or may not have actually happened, you'd think someone would write that I got Howard out. It kills me that this is the story you always get right."

Rohr, who possesses a wonderfully dry sense of humor, added that he had recently dropped a 40-foot putt and asked that it be included in this book. Told that it probably would not be included, he said, "But I'm sure if I missed a three-foot putt, that would be in there. That's how sportswriters work."

Rohr is always asked if a few plot twists here or there might have led to a no-hitter. He is quick to point out the pitch he threw to Howard *before* the single, called a ball by plate umpire Cal Drummond.

"I threw a 1-2 pitch to Ellie that everyone except the plate umpire knew was a strike," said Rohr. "(Catcher) Russ Gibson knew it was a strike and Ellie knew it was a strike. The ump's hand kind of went halfway up, but not all the way up. And then Ellie singled to right."

Then there was the trip to the mound by Red Sox manager Dick Williams with two out in the ninth. Rohr, sufficiently nervous already, didn't need his manager to come out to the mound to remind him what was at stake. And Williams agrees. In his book, *No More Mr. Nice Guy: A Life of Hardball*, co-authored by Bill Plaschke, the former manager writes: "I've beaten myself over the head about that trip to the mound . . . he had one shot at fame, and my meddling may have helped blow it for him."

To add to the poignancy of Rohr's one-hitter, it was one of only three games the lefthander won during his brief major-league career. He would beat the Yankees again a week later at Fenway Park, but his only other big-league victory was with the Cleveland Indians a year later.

His arm was sore and his time was up. He kicked around the minors with the Detroit Tigers, and then the Montreal Expos, and then he went home to California to get on with his life. He was 24 years old.

"The day my career ended was the day I enrolled in law school," Rohr said. "I decided I wasn't going to give myself a chance to feel sorry for myself. This isn't to say I didn't miss baseball. It took a long time to get it out of my system. It was a good three years before I could watch a game on television, and five years before I could even attend a game.

Photo courtesy of Billy Rohr

"I'm comfortable with it now, but it was not always so," he said. "Because I was not done when I was done. Mentally, I had several more seasons in me. But now it's ok."

After his baseball career ended, Rohr, who was born and raised in California and studied at Cerritos College, enrolled at the law school at Western State University in Fullerton. Today, he is a medical malpractice defense attorney in San Bernadino, working closely with Loma Linda University Medical Center.

He has a daughter, Carla, from his first marriage. And Carla has twin boys, Luke and Jack. He also has a stepdaughter, Kristie, from his second marriage to Kathy, herself a lawyer.

"Neither one of us could get honest work when we got out of prison," Rohr joked. "So we both became lawyers."